BAPTIZING
Harry Potter

BAPTIZING
Harry Potter

A Christian Reading of J. K. Rowling

Luke Bell

HiddenSpring

Cover and book design by Lynn Else

Library of Congress Cataloging-in-Publication Data

Bell, Luke.
    Baptizing Harry Potter : a Christian reading of J.K. Rowling / by Luke Bell.
        p. cm.
    ISBN 978-1-58768-058-8 (alk. paper)
    1. Rowling, J. K.—Religion. 2. Christianity in literature. 3. Children—Books and reading. 4. Potter, Harry (Fictitious character) I. Title.
    PR6068.O93Z536 2010
    823´.914—dc22

                                                            2010000266

Published by
HiddenSpring
an imprint of Paulist Press
997 Macarthur Boulevard
Mahwah, New Jersey 07430

www.hiddenspringbooks.com

Printed and bound in the
United States of America

Contents

For my godson, Aelred

Acknowledgments

I am grateful to the many people with whom I have discussed the Harry Potter stories, particularly Alice Clackson, Duncan Smith, and Katherine and Andrew Tulloch, who helped this book considerably with corrections and suggestions. My thanks are also due to Paul McMahon of Paulist Press for his encouragement during the writing of it.

Last, but obviously not least, I must thank the person who made this book possible and who has enabled people throughout the world to make connections with each other by giving them a shared narrative: J. K. Rowling.

Preface

I suppose everyone has their story of how they first came to read Harry Potter. I was in Carlisle, a city in the north of England. I was staying with a friend who was about to get married. I was his best man. He had a lot to do—he hadn't even written his speech for the wedding—and I was left to my own devices. On the bookshelves, I saw a copy of *Harry Potter and the Philosopher's Stone*. (It was renamed *Harry Potter and the Sorcerer's Stone* in the United States.) I began to read it. Within an hour, somehow the world in it seemed more important to me than the one that normally claimed my attention. I felt I had discovered an author who spoke to me personally in a very special way. I did not particularly imagine others would feel the same.

But of course others did feel the same: millions of them. Some of those others have shared with me the experience of reading the books as they came out. This book is shaped by their insights, as well as my own. Our experience of growing up, of learning, and of facing life—and death—has found an articulation in these books that reveals to us something touching, important, and memorable about its meaning. They speak of our common experience.

However, there is something I do not have in common with most of the people with whom I have discussed the books. And it gives me my own angle on the stories.

I am a monk. I have dedicated my life to what is beyond what can normally be seen. I live for the supernatural. I have a calling. I did not receive a letter in an envelope made of yellowish parchment, with the address written in emerald-green ink.[1] Nonetheless, I have a sense of calling to this abbey where I live, which I have described in another book.[2] Here I want to share something that perhaps my calling helps me to be aware of: a sense of the spiritual values in the Harry Potter books.

I am not arguing that the books were written to promote the Christian faith. However, I do believe that the Christian faith speaks about what is most fundamental in the human condition. Good writing does the same, so it is to be expected that there is common ground. Furthermore, these books are written in a tradition that is much molded by the Christian faith. I do not believe that because they describe magic, they are doing the devil's work. This commonly heard objection is one that I shall consider in due course.

However, I do not think it likely that you are reading this book to settle this question in your mind. I imagine you have already read the Harry Potter books. If you have not, I do have a warning for you. The books, at least on a first reading, depend very much on a sense of surprise. And they are so intricately interwoven that I cannot comment intelligently on them without mentioning what happens in the end. I don't want to spoil the surprise for you, so please read them first.

This book is about the Harry Potter books, but I think you could probably understand it if you have seen all the movies. It is written to share my understanding and enjoyment of the series. It is a continuation of the conversations that I, and perhaps you, have had in the years since first reading *Harry Potter and the Philosopher's Stone*.

My friend and his bride, who were the ones who introduced me to Harry Potter, now have four children. I am godfather to the second of them, Aelred. Like Albus Severus, he belongs to a new generation that needs to make choices for itself, at the same time coming to terms with choices that others before them have made. This book is dedicated to him. It's not exactly a Firebolt, Aelred, but I hope you like it anyway.

Notes

1. *The Philosopher's Stone*, 30.
2. *A Deep and Subtle Joy: Life at Quarr Abbey*, Hidden-Spring/Gracewing, 2006.

Sequential List of Titles in the Harry Potter Series

1. *Harry Potter and the Philosopher's Stone*, London, Bloomsbury Publishing, 1997 (published in the United States under the title *Harry Potter and the Sorcerer's Stone*, New York, Scholastic, 1998).
2. *Harry Potter and the Chamber of Secrets*, London, Bloomsbury Publishing, 1998.
3. *Harry Potter and the Prisoner of Azkaban*, London, Bloomsbury Publishing, 1999.
4. *Harry Potter and the Goblet of Fire*, London, Bloomsbury Publishing, 2000.
5. *Harry Potter and the Order of the Phoenix*, London, Bloomsbury Publishing, 2003.
6. *Harry Potter and the Half-Blood Prince*, London, Bloomsbury Publishing, 2005.
7. *Harry Potter and the Deathly Hallows*, London, Bloomsbury Publishing, 2007.

Please note that all page references are to the UK edition; also that extracts from those books retain their original British spelling.

1

The Scope and Tragedy of the Thing

THE STRUCTURE OF THE SERIES

"We did it, we bashed them, wee Potter's the One,
And Voldy's gone mouldy, so now let's have fun!"

So sings Peeves when Voldemort is defeated, while Ron Weasley comments, with characteristic irony: "Really gives a feeling for the scope and tragedy of the thing, doesn't it?"[1] This chapter attempts to improve upon Peeves' assessment of the scope of the series by examining its structure. The tragic aspect of the narrative comes, of course, from the evil Voldemort, whose very name indicates that he wants death. Evidently he wants the death of others—above all, that of Harry Potter—but at a more fundamental level, as we shall see, he chooses the death of his own soul, what the Bible calls "the second death."[2] The scope of the narrative is Voldemort's return to power and his being confronted, particularly by Harry.

THE TURNING POINT OF THE STORY

In J. K. Rowling's Harry Potter series (I'll refer to her as JK from here on), the pivotal point of the whole story is in chapter 32 of the fourth book, *Harry Potter and the Goblet of Fire*, when Voldemort takes on a body. Up to this point, he is acting either through others (Books 1 and 3) or through a Horcrux (Book 2). After this point, he becomes a murderous force to be reckoned with. Before this point, the only death is that of his agent Quirrell, for whom little sympathy is felt, and the death is not directly described.[3] After this point, there is a death of a significantly sympathetic character in each volume, starting with Cedric Diggory in Book 4, and ending with many such deaths in Book 7.

This makes Book 4 the pivotal book of the series. Not only is it the middle book of the series—the chronicle of the middle year of Harry's association with Hogwarts—it is also the book in which everything changes. Before Voldemort rises again, the playful aspect of the magic at Hogwarts is uppermost. After it, everybody faces "dark and difficult times," as Dumbledore says.[4]

The change is abrupt. When I first read this book, blind to the clues that are obvious on a second reading, I felt—until that critical change—that it was about ordinary school life, and even wondered if the author, now that she was both successful and happily married, had an attenuated sense of the dark side of life. The Triwizard-Cup-turned-Portkey jerked me out of that view, as it jerked Harry and Cedric out of Hogwarts,[5] and I realized that the Dark forces were more sinister for being so well hidden.

Book 4 divides Harry's prepubertal life at Hogwarts from his postpubertal life there. It is the book in which the boy/girl thing enters the story in earnest. There is comedy in this, which is well brought out in the movie, but the more important change in his life is that Harry has to start facing serious evil as a grown-up. Books 1 to 3 are, as it were, play: a rehearsal for what will come in adulthood. Books 5 to 7 are a battle against evil in earnest. The first three books are obviously children's books. Books 5 to 7 are much less obviously so. In the first three books, the ways of the magical world, and such details as the rules of Quidditch, are explained each time; after that, the reader is expected to know them. Evil in the first half of the series is something that can be laughed at. Its relentless focus on the self has expression in Gilderoy Lockhart's comical self-assessment as "magical me."[6] In the second half of the series, the pile of bodies in the sculpture at the Ministry of Magic ominously expresses a self-assertion that is given expression in the far-from-funny slogan "Magic is might."[7] *Harry Potter and the Order of the Phoenix*, which begins the more grown-up phase of Harry's life, has the greatest focus on his adolescence. "He's not a child!" says Sirius. "He's not an adult either!" says Mrs. Weasley.[8] When the book begins, Harry has "the unhealthy look of someone who has grown a lot in a short space of time."[9] He is very different from the Harry of the first book, who is "small and skinny for his age."[10] It is as though the story is beginning again.

THE PATTERN OF THE STORY

And in a way, the story *is* beginning again; it is just in the reverse order. Book 4 divides the series. Books 5, 6, and 7 mirror, respectively, Books 3, 2, and 1. The structure is chiasmic. The pattern is ABCDCBA. As the writing on the Golden Snitch says, "I open at the close."[11] There are multiple connections between the opening chapter of the first book and the close of the whole thing in the last book.

Dumbledore's Put-Outer that is used to plunge Privet Drive into darkness[12] is bequeathed to Ron under its grown-up name of Deluminator;[13] Hagrid arrives on Sirius's motorbike (also featured in the prequel) to deliver Harry,[14] and in the last book takes him away again on the same motorbike.[15] In the first chapter of the first book we are told that "when he couldn't kill Harry Potter, Voldemort's power somehow broke—and that's why he's gone."[16] And at the end of the last book, Voldemort's power is finally broken and he is gone for good when, for the last time, he cannot kill Harry Potter.[17] The difference is that Harry, like the name for the Put-Outer, has become grown-up. The series is about that growth.

Other links between the first book and the last speak of it. In the first book a mere agent of Voldemort's, Quirrell, dies.[18] In the last book Voldemort himself dies:[19] a defeat that only a grown wizard could accomplish. In the first book Harry is wrong to think that Snape is against him.[20] Snape is, in fact, protecting him from Dark Magic. In the last book Harry learns this lesson again, as he discovers that Snape sent his Patronus to protect him against Dark Magic,[21] but this time Harry accepts it maturely and allows it to become so rooted in his heart that he gives his own son Snape's name.[22] This is a maturity that failed him when he was under threat at the beginning of his adolescence, and did not realize that Snape, as a member of the Order of the Phoenix, could have helped him.[23] Only at its close does he understand fully what he first knew at the opening of his life at Hogwarts. The whole Snape theme—endlessly discussed by Harry, Ron, and Hermione throughout the series—is topped and tailed by a parallel plot twist, which, remarkably, is able to fool the first-time reader both times.

However, by far the most momentous connection between the first and last book is that which speaks of the greatest growth in Harry. In the first book we are told of the protection that his mother's sacrifice—her willingness to lay down her life—gives Harry.[24] In the last book Harry himself makes that same sacrifice, or "meant to, and that's what did it,"[25] and so gives protection to others; for example, Neville, who is able to break free from Voldemort's Body-Bind Curse, seizes the Sword of Gryffindor from the Sorting Hat and kills Nagini.[26] This is a growth from receiving sacrificial love to giving it.

The second and sixth books are linked in ways that parallel the link between Books 1 and 7. There are objects that connect them. In Book 2 Harry hides in a cabinet in Borgin and Burkes, a shop in Knockturn Alley.[27] This is the cabinet through which the Death Eaters enter Hogwarts in Book 6.[28] In the same shop, in the same episode in Book 2, he spots "a magnificent necklace of opals" with a note saying, "*Caution: Do Not Touch. Cursed—Has Claimed the Lives of Nineteen Muggle Owners to Date.*"[29] This is the necklace that almost kills Katie Bell in Book 6.[30]

There is also a link between Books 2 and 6 that concerns growth: that of Ginny. She is a major character in both books. In Book 2, she does not think, as Riddle scornfully says, that "famous, good, great Harry Potter would *ever* like her."[31] Riddle is able to exploit her fears and vulnerability to work through her.[32] In Book 6, she is a changed person. Following some handy tips from Hermione, she becomes more independent from Harry and wins from him the love she has always wanted.[33]

Ginny's letting go of Harry enables her to win him. This is the playing in a minor key of the gospel theme of losing one's life to find it. The corollary, "those who want to save their life will lose it,"[34] is a theme linking Books 2 and 6 that is played in a major key. This gospel paradox is given expression in the evil magic of making a Horcrux: splitting one's soul by murder so as to keep a bit of it in an object.[35] The diary that Riddle uses to possess Ginny in Book 2 is one of the Horcruxes that he makes, which we find out about in Book 6.[36] This attempt to keep his life leads him to lose his true life, as it invests his soul in the material instead of leaving it free and whole. His soul becomes vulnerable by this investment.[37]

Books 3 and 5, like the other pairs in the chiasmic structure, are linked by a character: that of Sirius Black. In Book 3, Harry finds with him a bond that is the nearest thing he knows to having a parent.[38] Sirius becomes a valued mentor to him. In Book 5 Harry's love for Sirius leads him to put himself in danger, a danger from which Sirius comes to rescue him at the cost of his life. Yet this sacrifice brings Voldemort into the open and begins the confrontation that is his ultimate downfall.

SIGNIFICANT VARIATION IN THE STORY

Love and sacrifice are key themes in the series; they will be considered in greater depth in a later chapter. But there is one reflection of the theme of sacrificial love that is in the structure itself of the series, and so merits mention now. Each of the books follows a pattern: there is, at the beginning, Harry's birthday, the journey to Hogwarts, and the sorting; and, at the end of the academic year, a talk between Dumbledore and Harry about the meaning of the latter's experiences, the end of term assembly, and the journey from Hogwarts. As with musical themes, or metrical form in poetry, there are variations in this pattern, and they have significance.

At the end of Book 6 there is no talk with Dumbledore and no end-of-year assembly. He is dead. In Book 7,

Hogwarts, of which he is the life and soul, is absent from the main narrative until the closing chapters. Dumbledore does talk with Harry at the end of this final book, but from beyond the tomb. Book 6 is the darkest book of the series—it prompted a friend of mine to write to me that it was no longer a children's story. At the end of Book 7 the victory over the One Who Wants Death is won, albeit at great cost, and it is celebrated as the sun rises. This pattern in the last two books points, at least for a monk who is accustomed to celebrate it in the liturgical rhythm of each year, to the ultimate sacrifice of Christ on the cross and his resurrection from the dead on Easter morning. Book 6 is in some sense the story of Good Friday, Book 7 the story of Holy Saturday. Of course, Dumbledore is flawed—we cannot simply say he is Christ—but his death in Book 6 reflects the loss experienced by those first students of the supernatural, commonly called the disciples, and his absence from Hogwarts in Book 7, as well as the general bleakness in the magical world, seem to speak of the emptiness of Holy Saturday. Thus the wonderful dawn that comes at the end of Book 7, following Harry's encounter with Voldemort, and coinciding with a victorious Harry being shown to be alive when he was thought to be dead, is redolent of the story of the Lord's resurrection on Easter morning.[39]

There are other links between JK's story and the foundational story of the Christian tradition that suggest that God's ultimate divine sacrifice and love are indeed reflected in the series. These links will be examined in what follows. Here, suffice it to say that the very structure of the series already speaks of this. The patterning is full of meaning. It is "something of great constancy,"[40] and the seven books are wonderfully interwoven. And seven is a magic number, of course.[41]

Notes

1. *The Deathly Hallows*, 598.

2. Revelation 20:14. Unless otherwise indicated, quotations from the Bible are from the New Revised Standard Version.

3. *The Philosopher's Stone*, 216. As mentioned earlier, the first book in the series was published in the United Kingdom under the title *Harry Potter and the Philosopher's Stone*. For the U.S. edition, which appeared a year later, the title was changed to *Harry Potter and the Sorcerer's Stone*. Because all page references here are to the British edition, *Philosopher's Stone* is used throughout this book.

4. *The Goblet of Fire*, 627.

5. *The Goblet of Fire*, 551.

6. *The Chamber of Secrets*, 48.

7. *The Deathly Hallows*, 198.

8. *The Order of the Phoenix*, 84.

9. *The Order of the Phoenix*, 7.

10. *The Philosopher's Stone*, 20.

11. *The Deathly Hallows*, 113.

12. *The Philosopher's Stone*, 12.

13. *The Deathly Hallows*, 106.

14. *The Philosopher's Stone*, 16.

15. *The Deathly Hallows*, 50–51.

16. *The Philosopher's Stone*, 15.

17. *The Deathly Hallows*, 596.

18. *The Philosopher's Stone*, 216.

19. *The Deathly Hallows*, 596.

20. *The Philosopher's Stone*, 209.

21. *The Deathly Hallows*, 551–53.

22. *The Deathly Hallows*, 607.

23. *The Order of the Phoenix*, 655.

24. *The Philosopher's Stone*, 216.

25. *The Deathly Hallows*, 591.

26. *The Deathly Hallows*, 587.
27. *The Chamber of Secrets*, 42.
28. *The Half-Blood Prince*, 548.
29. *The Chamber of Secrets*, 44.
30. *The Half-Blood Prince*, 233–36.
31. *The Chamber of Secrets*, 228.
32. *The Chamber of Secrets*, 228–29.
33. *The Half-Blood Prince*, 603, 499.
34. Luke 9:24.
35. *The Half-Blood Prince*, 464–67.
36. *The Half-Blood Prince*, chapter 23.
37. *The Deathly Hallows*, 90.
38. *The Order of the Phoenix*, 726.
39. *The Deathly Hallows*, 595.
40. Shakespeare, *A Midsummer Night's Dream*, act 5, scene 1, line 26.
41. *The Half-Blood Prince*, 470.

2

More Things in Heaven and Earth

GOING BEYOND THE NORMAL

In Shakespeare's play *Hamlet*, Horatio cries out on see-ing the ghost, "This is wondrous strange!" Hamlet responds:

And therefore, as a stranger give it welcome.
There are more things in heaven and earth, Horatio,
Than are dreamt of in your philosophy.[1]

JK is, in a way, saying the same thing in the Harry Potter series. She is inviting us to imagine that there can be some-thing beyond what we take to be normal: ghosts, obviously,[2] but much more besides. She invites us to open our minds to what is beyond what we can perceive with our senses. In doing this, she puts before us the possibility of the spiritual. Any teaching about spiritual values needs to postulate that there is a reality beyond the mundanely material. If there is only the material, the spiritual does not exist.

The series begins with a challenge to the normal; it goes on to show people acting in a sacrificial way, for which they can expect no reward in this world. Toward the end, it shows us Dumbledore, who clearly concedes that he is dead, and yet who enjoys a life much greater than that of any ghost's "feeble imitation of life."[3] In other words, the series shows us a world in which there can be spiritual values.

This chapter deals with the challenge to the normal: the idea that there is more than is dreamt of in our mundane philosophy. Other chapters, later in the book, will deal with such large questions as those of sacrifice and life after death.

In a way, now that the series is complete, it is difficult to think about it as challenging the normal. After all, we have become used to thinking of what happens in the books as normal, at least normal for the world of Hogwarts. True, there may be some things we find difficult to believe—for me, it is the Knight Bus;[4] for one of my brethren, it is Ron speaking Parseltongue.[5] But the very fact that these things stand out for us indicates the scope of JK's achievement in getting us to believe that almost everything she writes about is ordinary, and not weird and fantastical. Before she wrote, we could not have imagined it.

There is something of a parallel to this in the monastery, where we take for granted that there is a world beyond this one: that there is heaven, that there are angels and saints, and so on. We can forget that this is not obvious to everyone, and, indeed, that there may have been a time even for some of us when it was not taken for granted that these things are so. The moment of coming to faith can slip from the mind.

Dursley Dullness

However, we can recover a sense of how JK first challenged the idea that there could be more than what we think of us as normal by going back to the first paragraph of the series:

> Mr. and Mrs. Dursley, of Number Four, Privet Drive, were proud to say that they were perfectly normal, thank you very much. They were the last people you'd expect to be involved in anything strange or mysterious, because they just didn't hold with such nonsense.[6]

The Dursleys, when the strange and mysterious comes into their lives, do not "as a stranger, give it welcome." To them, illness is a sign of "something foreign for tea."[7] The reader's mind is opened up to the possibility of "more things in heaven and earth" by the ludicrousness of the Dursleys' attempts to resist the strange and mysterious. This process is helped by the unattractiveness of the Dursleys. Mr. Dursley is boring. Boring is his business: he is the director of a firm that makes drills. He picks out his most boring tie for work.[8] We are told, of his dinner guests, that he "bored them all with a long talk about Grunnings, his drill-making company."[9]

If I reflect on my own experience of finding people boring, I find that the factor they have in common is their lack of receptivity. They are not open to anything new. Their talk tends to be without pause: they do not leave a space for anything to be received from the one to whom they are talking. They do not relate to the other. They have no capacity for wonder. They have decided how the world is, and their mental picture of it is not open to question. Further input is unwelcome.

The Dursleys fit this characterization of boring people: they hate Harry's asking questions, but even more they hate "his talking about anything acting in a way it shouldn't."[10]

They hate and despise magic.[11] Mr. Dursley (more so than Mrs. Dursley) is obsessively opposed to the strange and mysterious entering his world. His response to magical letters arriving at 4 Privet Drive is to nail up the letter box. He implies that the senders are deranged, although his attempt to use a piece of fruitcake to knock in a nail suggests that he may be a bit nutty himself. The strange and mysterious is not so easily stopped, however: even boarding up the cracks around the front and back doors does not stop the letters from arriving.[12] Nor does staying at a hotel.[13] And going to a remote, storm-stricken island only leads to the arrival of a personal representative of the magical world.[14]

Although his attempts to do so are spectacularly unsuccessful, Vernon Dursley wants to block out all that is strange and mysterious—all that is magical. He wants to stamp magic out of Harry.[15] Even saying the word *magic* in a nonmagical context produces an explosion from him. To him it is an "abnormality."[16] His wish to keep Harry totally away from such things is indicated by his choice of school for Harry—Stonewall High.[17] He wants to put a high stone wall between him and the magical world. This implication of the school's name becomes clear in Book 5, when Harry reflects that the arrival of Dementors in the town of Little Whinging seems "to have breached the great, invisible wall that divided the relentlessly non-magical world of Privet Drive and the world beyond."[18]

WEASLEY WONDER

Harry belongs in "the world beyond." The ambiguity of the phrase suggests not only the magical world, but the world of the spirit: the world of values that are not merely material. And, appropriately, this world is represented for him in a particular way by a very poor family. The Burrow, home to the Weasleys, is as higgledy-piggledy and untidy as 4 Privet Drive is straight and tidy, but Harry thinks it "brilliant."[19] The sheer wildness of its strange and mysterious magic is depicted by a scene in which Bill and Charlie both have their wands out and are making two battered old tables fly high above the lawn and smash into each other, each brother attempting to knock the other's out of the air, to the cheers of Fred and George and the laughter of Ginny.[20] This world literally bursts into the living room of the Dursleys, with the arrival there of "Mr. Weasley, Fred, George, and Ron in a cloud of rubble and loose chippings."[21] It is antithetical to the Dursleys' world, and what to the Dursleys is normal is alien to the Weasleys. Ron comments, "I think Mum's got a second cousin who's an accountant, but we never talk about him."[22] The merely monetary is not celebrated where openness to the wonderful prevails.

However, it is too simple to say that openness to the wonderful prevails everywhere beyond the wall that separates the nonmagical from the magical. The same drama of restriction and closed-mindedness fighting the exuberant welcome of the wonderful is played out within the magical world as well. For example, Professor Umbridge wants to limit her students' engagement with magic to "theoretical knowledge." Harry complains, "She's not letting us use magic at all!" And Ron says, "All we do is read the stupid textbook." Umbridge has closed her mind to the strange, referring contemptuously to "extremely dangerous half-breeds."[23] She is the drafter of a bit of anti-werewolf legislation; she loathes part-humans and campaigns to have merpeople rounded up and tagged.[24]

Against her attempt to limit existence to some notion of what is normal, it is once again the Weasleys who take up arms: this time Fred and George in particular. As with the intrusion into the Dursleys' living room, there is a sense of the breaking-in of an exuberant wildness that cannot be contained. The intrusion is pyrotechnic. It is described in a single, long sentence, whose failure to stop is mimetic of the uncontrollability of the fireworks:

> Dragons comprised entirely of green and gold sparks were soaring up and down the corridors, emitting loud fiery blasts and bangs as they went; shocking-pink Catherine wheels five feet in diameter were whizzing lethally through the air like so many flying saucers; rockets with long tails of brilliant silver stars were ricocheting off the walls; sparklers were writing swear words in midair of their own accord; firecrackers were exploding like mines everywhere Harry looked, and instead of burning themselves out, fading from sight or fizzling to a halt, these pyrotechnical miracles seemed to be gaining in energy and momentum the longer he watched.[25]

The increase in energy and momentum recalls the way the letters to 4 Privet Drive increase in number the more attempts are made to stop them,[26] and, indeed, the fireworks operate analogously: every attempt to Vanish them makes them multiply by ten.[27] This dynamic suggests the overwhelming reality of what is strange, mysterious, and wonderful; what is in "the world beyond."[28] The fireworks cannot be dismissed as simple insubordination, or even as the charismatic taking over from the hierarchical, since the deputy headmistress, Professor McGonagall, like the other teachers, doesn't seem to mind them very much. "Dear, dear," she says sardonically, as one of the dragons soars around her classroom, emitting loud bangs and exhaling flame.[29] They are magic: strange, mysterious, and wonderful.

AND STRANGER STILL...

Yet, even by this standard, there is stranger still. JK achieves the extraordinary feat of creating a character who is strange in the context of strangeness, who seeks strangeness beyond this strangeness: Xenophilius Lovegood.[30] His first name (from the Greek) means "lover of the strange." If we put it in parallel with his second name, JK is making a statement to the effect that the strange is good. In one sense, this is a welcoming of the wonder of magic, but it is also in line with the drift of the whole series against discrimination. Failure to welcome the strange is associated with the nastiness of Umbridge and her hatred of half-breeds, her callousness toward house-elves, and her murderous indifference toward Muggles and Mudbloods. Ironically, Hermione, a Mudblood herself and the greatest champion of house-elf rights, is the one who finds it most difficult to go along with Xenophilius's love of the strange. She is skeptical about the Deathly Hallows, which, "if united, will make the possessor master of Death." Xenophilius finds her "painfully limited. Narrow. Close-minded."[31]

In fact, the Deathly Hallows do turn out to exist, and Harry becomes possessor of them. He is the master of death—at least in the spiritual sense of not letting the apparent certainty of his own death frighten him into abandoning what is right: facing Lord Voldemort, the One Who Wants Death literally for others and spiritually for himself. And the Hallows do, in fact, enable this. The Resurrection Stone evokes the presence of those who have gone "on"[32] before, whose encouragement gives Harry the bravery he needs to face death.[33] The Invisibility Cloak gives him the cover he needs to get past the people who would discourage him from going to his death.[34] And his mastery of the Elder Wand turns its Killing Curse against him back toward Voldemort.[35] In the immediate, literal sense, Harry does survive death too; although the fundamental contrast that is being made is not between his survival and Voldemort's death. It is between his willingness to die and the fullness of his spiritual life, and Voldemort's obsessive unwillingness to die and his spiritual death. Dumbledore makes this contrast when he tells Harry that he has less to fear from return to the realm beyond death than Voldemort has.[36] It is the gospel theme, already mentioned, of losing one's life to find it and those wanting to save their life losing it.[37]

Being right about the strange does not make Xenophilius a more admirable character than Hermione. She retains the Gryffindor quality of courage that makes her unyielding in the struggle against Voldemort, while Xenophilius does give in to Voldemort's cruel pressure and allows himself to be used in the fight against Harry. And he is a ludicrous character. Ron, who stands for (in the magical context) a common-sense, down-to-earth, plain-speaking view of things, finds his voice shaking with the strain of not laughing when he joins in with Xenophilius' conversation with Hermione.[38] And, of course, Hermione is right about the Erumpent Horn.[39]

MAGIC GOOD AND BAD

Making the strange welcome opens up the possibility of the spiritual, but that is not itself enough. Magic is strange and wonderful, but it is not necessarily good. Indeed, there are those who argue that the Harry Potter books should not be read at all, because magic is necessarily bad. This ignores the particular way in which JK uses magic: what it means in her books. The current practice of calling good things "wicked" does not, in fact, make them bad. It is possible to express a spiritual tradition without using the language of that tradition. For example, in *Till We Have Faces*, C. S. Lewis uses the language of Greek mythology to convey the Christian spiritual tradition. In *King Lear*, Shakespeare pictures the events of the play in a pagan context, so much so that less-perceptive critics have taken it to present an atheistic view; yet it can be read as a powerful restatement of the Christian spiritual tradition, as encapsulated in the first beatitude: "Blessed are the poor in spirit, for theirs is the kingdom of heaven."[40] Similarly, in the Harry Potter series, the language of magic articulates the values of the Christian tradition.

This language is used to describe some acts that are straightforwardly those of Christian charity. Kingsley Shacklebolt, broadcasting on *Potterwatch*, speaks of "truly inspirational stories of wizards and witches risking their own safety to protect Muggle friends and neighbours, often without the Muggles' knowledge." Further, he urges listeners "to emulate their example, perhaps by casting a protective charm over any Muggle dwellings in your street. Many lives could be saved if such simple measures are taken."[41] Harry makes a charitable donation in favor of the magical care of the sick, to the amount of the whole contents of his money bag.[42]

But the language of magic is also used to describe acts of great evil. There are ways of distinguishing the two. I am reminded of the rule of thumb an exorcist I knew had: if spiritual power was used to gain a partial advantage against the common good, it was to be fought. The realm of the spiritual is not to be identified simply with what is good.

Cornelius Fudge, who does not always see and speak clearly about things, sees at least this much. When the Muggle Prime Minister thinks that magic alone is the answer to the problems they face, saying "You can do *magic*! Surely you can sort out—well—*anything*!" Fudge responds, "The trouble is, the other side can do magic too, Prime Minister!"[43]

The battle between the two sides, what C. S. Lewis calls "The Great Battle," is a major theme of the Harry Potter series. By it, JK articulates spiritual values, and shows the attractiveness of the good. It is the subject of the next chapter.

Notes

1. Act 1, scene 5, lines 164–67.
2. *The Philosopher's Stone*, 86.
3. *The Deathly Hallows*, 567, and *The Order of the Phoenix*, 759.
4. *The Prisoner of Azkaban*, 30.
5. *The Deathly Hallows*, 501.
6. *The Philosopher's Stone*, 7.
7. *The Order of the Phoenix*, 28.
8. *The Philosopher's Stone*, 7.
9. *The Prisoner of Azkaban*, 25.
10. *The Philosopher's Stone*, 24.
11. *The Goblet of Fire*, 23.
12. *The Philosopher's Stone*, 34.
13. *The Philosopher's Stone*, 36.
14. *The Philosopher's Stone*, 39.
15. *The Philosopher's Stone*, 43.
16. *The Chamber of Secrets*, 7–8.
17. *The Philosopher's Stone*, 28.
18. *The Order of the Phoenix*, 39.
19. *The Chamber of Secrets*, 29.

20. *The Goblet of Fire*, 57.
21. *The Goblet of Fire*, 41–43.
22. *The Philosopher's Stone*, 75.
23. *The Order of the Phoenix*, 219.
24. *The Order of the Phoenix*, 271.
25. *The Deathly Hallows*, 557.
26. *The Philosopher's Stone*, chapter 3.
27. *The Order of the Phoenix*, 558.
28. *The Order of the Phoenix*, 39.
29. *The Order of the Phoenix*, 558.
30. *The Deathly Hallows*, 117 and chapter 20.
31. *The Deathly Hallows*, 333.
32. *The Deathly Hallows*, 578.
33. *The Deathly Hallows*, 560–61.
34. *The Deathly Hallows*, 558.
35. *The Deathly Hallows*, 595–96.
36. *The Deathly Hallows*, 578.
37. Luke 9:24.
38. *The Deathly Hallows*, 333.
39. *The Deathly Hallows*, 325 and 340.
40. Matthew 5:3. The argument about *King Lear* is made in chapter 10 of my book *Paradise on Earth: Exploring a Christian Response to Suffering* (Stowmarket, UK: Kevin Mayhew Publishers, 1993).
41. *The Deathly Hallows*, 357.
42. *The Order of the Phoenix*, 118 and 142.
43. *The Half-Blood Prince*, 24.

3

As If a Man Were
Author of Himself

GOOD AGAINST EVIL

"No one is good but God alone," says the gospel.[1] In line with this, JK does not set any single character before us as being good in an unqualified way. Those who come to fight on the side of good do so as the culmination of a process of growth toward the good. James, Dumbledore, Sirius, Snape, Harry, Ron, and Hermione all have their flaws and weaknesses, and they all grow into their roles as warriors for the good. Lily, if we discount one childhood episode that shows less-than-perfect charity,[2] is the one character who does not seem to have much of a past that she has had to grow beyond in order to be what she is. However, perhaps we are seeing her through Harry's eyes and with the assumption that mothers are good as such, and we do not see a lot of her. Dobby fights heroically on the side of good, but his earlier attempts to do good—such as bewitching the Bludger to knock Harry off his broomstick[3]—are maladroit to the point of having a reverse effect to that intended.

BAPTIZING Harry Potter

Goodness in the characters is something that is struggled toward, not something that is just given. However, it is taken as a given that human life in itself is good: "Every human life is worth the same, and worth saving."[4] This statement (by Kingsley Shacklebolt) is made in the context of the fight against the murderous discrimination of Voldemort and his Death Eaters, which suggests that the values that are in the Harry Potter series emerge from the conflict with, and by contrast with, what is evil. It is when we see Fred, dead and with "the ghost of his last laugh still etched upon his face,"[5] that we fully understand the poignant beauty of Fred and Angelina "dancing so exuberantly that people around them were backing away for fear of injury."[6] What is valuable becomes more apparent when it is attacked by what is evil. The Christian creed was defined in the struggle with heresy. So, in examining the primordial and fundamental theme of good and evil in these books, it makes sense to start by looking at the evil.

As C. S. Lewis pointed out in *Preface to Paradise Lost*, it is easier to write about what is below us than about what is above us, easier to depict that to which we are capable of sinking than that to which we aspire. So it is artistically prudent for JK to write about the gravely evil, while eschewing the portraiture of utter sanctity.

As sanctity has its holy mystery, so evil has its unholy mystery. Saint Paul calls it "the mystery of iniquity."[7] JK expresses this in the name of her most evil character: Riddle. In one sense the "riddle" is simply an anagram, as Harry discovers in the Chamber of Secrets, when Tom Riddle magically changes TOM MARVOLO RIDDLE into I AM LORD VOLDEMORT. His initial middle name suggests he wants to "mar"—to do harm—but in the transformation he wants death itself. That is what the malicious orphan boy grows into. He fashions himself "a new name."[8] He acts, in Shakespeare's telling phrase, "as if a man were author of himself, and knew no other kin."[9] He acts as if his father, whom he kills, did not exist. He acts as if God does not exist. The transformation of his name uncovers the mystery of Lord Voldemort's past, but the mystery of evil remains: Why is there such futility—for Riddle and for others? Why, indeed, is there death? The whole series is a coming to terms with these questions.

THE INCARNATION OF EVIL

When evil breaks in at the pivotal point of the series, chapter 32 of Book 4, Voldemort acquires flesh, blood, and bone. The manner of this acquisition tells us something about evil. It is dependent on good. The gospel saying holds true: "No one is good but God alone."[10] Evil depends, therefore, on God. Every evil act is a perverted version of something godly. Evil cannot be autonomous. Only God exists of himself; has, as theologians put it, aseity. Voldemort's solitariness, his lack of dependence on anyone, is a hollow and doomed echo of God's authentic aloneness, his divine self-sufficiency. And Voldemort's coming among his own is a hollow and doomed echo of God's coming among his own,[11] as related in the Christian tradition. This tradition says that God, in choosing to come into the world, receives the willing consent of the one whose flesh he is to take.

The angel Gabriel is sent to the Virgin Mary to announce God's purpose of incarnation, and her consent is: "Here am I, the servant of the Lord; let it be with me according to your word."[12] In the incarnation of his evil self, Voldemort blasphemously parodies this. Pettigrew (Wormtail) takes the place of the Blessed Virgin Mary; the difference between them indicates the hideous gap between the true good and this evil. Pettigrew is indeed petty. That is the direction in which he grows. He is a worm and no man, he is a rat among men. His equivalent consent to Voldemort is described thus:

> And now Wormtail was whimpering. He pulled a long, thin, shining silver dagger from inside his robes. His voice broke into petrified sobs. *"Flesh— of the servant—w-willingly given—you will—revive— your master."*[13]

His slicing off of his right hand is the gift of his flesh to Voldemort.[14] The Dark Lord has mockingly foretold this, saying, "I will allow you to perform an essential task for me, one that many of my followers would give their right hands to perform."[15] The self-mutilation of a man replaces the motherhood of a woman. Acting with the consent of the other, however, is not characteristic of evil, and Pettigrew, acting for Voldemort, takes blood from Harry against his will with the words:

> *"B-blood of the enemy...forcibly taken....You will... resurrect your foe."*[16]

This contrasts with the free consent given by Mary, on behalf of the human race, to the incarnation of God. It also contrasts with the central mystery of the Christian tradition: the resurrection of the Lord. Voldemort does rise again,[17] but unlike the Lord's, his resurrection brings death, not life for others. The Lord gives his body and blood that others may live,[18] Voldemort takes the body and blood of others so that he may live (though, by doing this he unknowingly gives protection to his enemy).[19] The Lord gives his spirit, the spirit that makes dry bones live;[20] he fulfills the promise, "I am going to open your graves and bring you up from your graves, O my people....I will put my spirit within you, and you shall live."[21] Voldemort (through Pettigrew) opens up a grave not to give spirit and life, but simply to take dry bone:

> The surface of the grave at Harry's feet cracked. Horrified, Harry watched as a fine trickle of dust rose into the air at Wormtail's command, and fell softly into the cauldron.[22]

The Lord who comes into the world is known by his heavenly Father for all eternity;[23] Voldemort's father is unconscious of his own part in his son's taking flesh, as Wormtail's incantation attests:

> *"Bone of the Father, unknowingly given, you will renew your son!"*

These words are addressed "to the night,"[24] evil's element; Christ the Lord is "the true light, which enlightens everyone."[25] Voldemort is "the Dark Lord."[26] He is a hideous inversion of the Lord of the Christian tradition. He wants to rule both wizards and Muggles—to dominate both the spiritual and the earthly, but at his end he cannot use the words of the risen and glorious Lord, "All authority in heaven and earth has been given to me. Go therefore and make disciples."[27] His end is banal, futile, and empty:

> Tom Riddle hit the floor with a mundane finality, his body feeble and shrunken, the white hands empty, the snake-like face vacant and unknowing.[28]

Unlike the risen and glorious Lord, whose "Spirit of truth...will teach...everything,"[29] Riddle (rightly refused a job at Hogwarts) and his life have nothing to teach:

"Of house-elves and children's tales, of love, loyalty and innocence, Voldemort knows and understands nothing. *Nothing*."[30]

GOOD AS THE MEASURE OF EVIL

Evil cannot be understood except by reference to good. By comparing it to good, we see it for what it is: a parasite, claiming for itself what belongs to good, while inverting the substance of it. The other characters in the novels, realistically flawed as they are, cannot embody this good: it comes from the tradition within which the author writes. That tradition is, fundamentally, Christian, and whether the story's allusions to it and reflections of it are conscious or not, it is the tradition that has formed the language and symbols with which the story is put together. It also forms the teaching and the values that are conveyed to Harry (and his fellow students) and to the readers of the books.

The books' depiction of evil helps to convey these values. We can see a significant indication of it in the fact mentioned above: that Voldemort knows nothing of children's tales. Since the Harry Potter books *are* children's tales (albeit, tales *of* children who grow up, *for* children who grow up), this means that he knows nothing of the story in which he acts. He is unaware of what is truly going on. He is unaware of that fundamental story of the tradition in which this story is situated: the story of the God who became a child, that we may enter heaven by becoming as children.[31]

This disconnectedness from the hallowed aspect of childhood is given its most graphic description in the picture of Voldemort just before he is put in the cauldron from which he will rise:

The thing Wormtail had been carrying had the shape of a crouched human child, except that Harry had never seen anything less like a child. It was hairless and scaly-looking, a dark, raw, reddish black. Its arms and legs were thin and feeble, and its face—no child alive ever had a face like that—was flat and snake-like, with gleaming red eyes.[32]

Voldemort is ugly in his clinging to life. Unlike Nicolas Flamel, hero of the chocolate frog card,[33] he cannot let go;[34] he cannot lose his life to find it.[35] He is snake-like, recalling the crafty serpent who led Eve, and so Adam, into evil.[36] As the *Daily Prophet* says, "Serpents are historically associated with evil-doers."[37] His red eyes signal danger and death. His face is most unchildlike. He totally lacks the winning trust that characterizes the child.

It is this lack of trust that marks Voldemort. He despises Harry's parents for their trust, thinking: "How stupid they were, and how trusting, thinking that their safety lay in friends, that weapons could be discarded even for moments."[38] He regrets even the slight trust he puts in others. He reflects, "It had been a grave mistake to trust Bellatrix and Malfoy: didn't their stupidity and carelessness prove how unwise it was, ever, to trust?"[39] From lack of trust follows lack of relationship, lack of love. As Dumbledore says, shortly before Voldemort's death, "He does not love."[40] The young Riddle shows this same lack of desire for connection with others. Dumbledore comments to Harry just after they have shared his earliest memory of Voldemort:

> "I hope you noticed Riddle's reaction when I mentioned that another shared his first name, 'Tom'?"
> Harry nodded.

"There he showed his contempt for anything that tied him to other people, anything that made him ordinary. Even then he wished to be different, separate, notorious. He shed his name, as you know, within a few short years of that conversation and created the mask of 'Lord Voldemort' behind which he has been hidden for so long.

"I trust that you also noticed that Tom Riddle was already highly self-sufficient, secretive and, apparently, friendless? He did not want help or companionship on his trip to Diagon Alley. He preferred to operate alone. The adult Voldemort is the same. You will hear many of his Death Eaters claiming that they are in his confidence, that they alone are close to him, even understand him. They are deluded. Lord Voldemort has never had a friend, nor do I believe that he has ever wanted one."[41]

Both as boy and as man, Riddle wants to be alone and aloof. This aloofness leads him to the mistaken supposition that only he has ever discovered the Room of Requirement.[42] He is therefore mistaken in thinking that his Horcrux is safe there. He claims the uniqueness that belongs to God alone. Anything that links him to others is shunned. He would be utterly out of place in that school of the Lord's service, a monastery: the Benedictine Rule promotes the virtue of humility by saying that a monk should do nothing but that which the common rule of the monastery and the example of the senior monks urge.[43]

Riddle is diabolically proud. He is unkind, not only in the obvious sense of being cruel, first of all to other children in the orphanage[44] and then to Muggle and wizard alike when he grows up, but also in the sense that he has cut himself off from his kind. He acknowledges no kin, no kind like him. In this he is the utter opposite of the Lord of Light whose incarnation he parodies. Jesus not only accepts Mary as his mother, but extends his bounds of kinship indefinitely: "Whoever does the will of my Father in heaven," he says, "is my brother and sister and mother."[45] And he gives his mother to his disciple.[46]

REFLECTIONS OF CHRIST

The incarnation of Christ hovers behind the Harry Potter story. There is not a lot of explicit Christianity in the series—Mad-Eye's eyeball is buried in a spot marked with a small cross[47] and Harry prays inwardly at one point[48]—but there is one Christian celebration that is repeatedly mentioned. In fact, it occurs in every book. That is Christmas.

In the first four books, Christmas is celebrated at Hogwarts: In the first book, Harry is given the Invisibility Cloak.[49] In the second, Hermione bursts into the boys' dormitory carrying presents,[50] and enchanted snow falls from the highly decorated ceiling of the Great Hall.[51] In the third, Harry is given his Firebolt.[52] And in the fourth, the Yule Ball takes place.[53] After that, in keeping with the general change in tone in the books, it gets more serious. In the fifth book, Christmas is celebrated at 12 Grimmauld Place; they visit the closed ward at Saint Mungo's and come to know the sad fate of Mr. and Mrs. Longbottom.[54] In the sixth book, Christmas—a very frosty one—is celebrated at the Burrow.[55] And in the seventh book, Harry and Hermione find themselves outside a church in Godric's Hollow where a Christmas Eve celebration is taking place.[56] The following day, Voldemort is defeated in an attempt to kill Harry and his scream of rage echoes "across the dark gardens over the church bells ringing in Christmas Day."⁵⁷ In Voldemort's view of the world, this date for his thwarting would be an accident. Yet the ultimate backstory, the Christmas story, is one of the defeat of evil by the birth of a baby boy.

Voldemort knows nothing of this narrative. He does not understand the dynamic of his own defeat. He thinks of Harry as "the boy who survived by accident."⁵⁸ However, Harry's survival as a baby echoes the survival by the baby Jesus of the murderous attack of King Herod.⁵⁹ Professor McGonagall says about Voldemort's attack on the Potters:

> "They're saying he tried to kill the Potters' son, Harry. But—he couldn't. He couldn't kill that little boy. No one knows why, or how, but they're saying that when he couldn't kill Harry Potter, Voldemort's power somehow broke—and that's why he's gone."⁶⁰

The breaking of Voldemort's power echoes the defeat of evil by the incarnation of the Lord of Life. The attack that diminishes Voldemort's power gives Harry a scar. This brings to mind what the prophet Isaiah says about the Suffering Servant, "By his bruises we are healed."⁶¹ Harry's wounding is the banishment of Voldemort. And the scar gives him an access to Voldemort's thoughts and feelings that enables him to know where he is and what he is doing—a knowledge that proves invaluable when it shows Harry that the final Horcrux is hidden at Hogwarts.⁶²

Ignoring for the moment the fact that Harry is a summer baby, we can further link him with the incarnation of the Lord of Light, by reflecting on his coming to 4 Privet Drive. Saint Paul writes about the Lord, "Though he was in the form of God, [he] did not regard equality with God as something to be exploited, but emptied himself, taking the form of a slave, being born in human likeness."[63] Harry, although he is a wizard with a wizard's powers, comes to live as a Muggle. Harry comes out of the magical world (here envisaged as the spiritual world) into the humble and humbling Muggle world on Sirius' motorbike and he returns to the magical world the same way. Of course, Harry is not the Lord of Light: he has his faults—his enmity toward Snape, for example, blinds him to the authentic nature of Snape's commitment to the Order of the Phoenix. Nonetheless, we can also apply to him what Saint Paul goes on to say: "And being found in human form, he humbled himself and became obedient to the point of death."[64] Harry is obedient to the point of death. He accepts "the incontrovertible truth, which was that he must die."[65] He nobly seeks out his apparently fatal confrontation with Voldemort.[66]

Voldemort's Perverted Version of Christ's Goodness

If there are several ways in which Harry's story is linked to the story of the incarnation of the Lord of Light, there are several ways in which Voldemort's story is an evil parody and distortion of that story. First of all, it is driven by the opposite of self-emptying humility: Voldemort claims, "I am much, much more than a man."[67] And it would seem that he would want to be more than God too: for him, one incarnation is not enough. The body that Voldemort takes from his father, Pettigrew, and Harry is in addition to other investments of his soul in matter: the Horcruxes. The Lord of Light takes a body to die for the salvation of the world; the Dark Lord creates Horcruxes in order to avoid dying so he can dominate the world. In doing so he commits "the supreme act of evil."[68] The Lord of Light dies that others may live; the Dark Lord aims to make himself "impossible to kill by murdering other people."[69] However, at the deeper level, he is damaging himself rather than others.

This point, an important aspect of the books' teaching about evil, is made by Hermione: "Whatever happens to your body, your soul will survive, untouched....But it is the other way round with a Horcrux. The fragment of soul inside it depends on its container, its enchanted body, for survival. It can't exist without it."[70] Whereas the way of the Lord of Light leads the souls of all who come to him to heaven, the way of the Dark Lord leads his soul alone to be bound to earth. Whereas the Lord of Light embodies integrity, wholeness, and the oneness of God, the Dark Lord tears himself to pieces in the course of his evil pursuit. "Killing rips the soul apart." Voldemort does this deliberately so as to "encase the torn portion."[71] Further, he thinks that being torn apart is better because it makes him stronger—as he imagines—to have his soul in more pieces. This shocks and outrages head teachers of Hogwarts, or at least their portraits.[72] It violates the wisdom of the magical world.

Dumbledore explains that he worked out what was happening by the effect on Voldemort: "Lord Voldemort had seemed to grow less human with the passing years, and the transformation he had undergone seemed to me to be explicable only if his soul was mutilated beyond the realms of what we might call usual evil."[73] While the path of the Lord of Light leads to becoming more fully human—the glory of God is man fully alive—the path of the Dark Lord leads him to become less human. Even finding out about Horcruxes makes "his handsome features...somehow, less human."[74] His soul becomes more unstable as a result of being ripped each time he makes a Horcrux.[75] With fragmentation, the darkness deepens.

HARRY'S QUEST FOR THE GOOD

Harry confronts the darkness; the values that he adopts and grows into are, implicitly, those of the Lord of Light. Yet, for both Harry and the reader, the books' lessons about good and evil are never given in the simplistic form of having "good guys" and "bad guys." In Quidditch, Harry is a Seeker—which is surely no accident—and just as he has to seek the Horcruxes, so he has to seek what is truly good. The Lord of Light says: "Seek, and you will find."[76] Harry has to look *beyond* what first comes to sight.

There are a number of oppositions that may at first appear to be presenting good and evil. But none of them gives the full truth. Here are a few examples.

At Harry's first discovery of the magical world—with its fun, excitement, and liberation from Little Whinging—it might seem to him that the magical is good and Muggle bad, yet it gradually becomes clear that this view is very close to the evil that he is called to fight. The stigmatization of his friend Hermione as a "Mudblood,"[77] the "really sick" Muggle-baiting that he witnesses at the Quidditch World Cup,[78] and the statue of "hundreds and hundreds of naked bodies, men, women, and children…pressed together to support the weight of the handsomely robed wizards"[79] are all pointers to the truth that the dividing line between good and evil is not the same as that between Muggle and wizard. In his happiness that everyone seems to like him at the Burrow,[80] Harry might easily believe that the Weasleys embody good and the Dursleys evil. Yet Percy Weasley turns out to be, while not exactly evil, most certainly a prat,[81] Petunia agrees to keep Harry safe against the wishes of her husband,[82] and Dudley himself says to Harry, "I don't think you're a waste of space"—which, coming from him, is like "I love you."[83]

A more likely opposition might seem to be between the Weasleys and the Malfoys. Draco makes the contrast, to his own family's advantage, on the first journey to Hogwarts,[84] perhaps aware of the rumors that Harry himself is a dark wizard around whom the Dark Lord's old followers could rally once more.[85] The name Malfoy (from the French) means "bad faith," so they are marked as not having the right value system. The clear difference between their values and the Weasleys' is brought out in the exchange between Lucius Malfoy and Arthur Weasley in Flourish and Blotts.[86] However, the Malfoys are not entirely evil. Mrs. Malfoy's love for her son is stronger in the end than her loyalty to Voldemort,[87] and Draco is not completely given over to evil. Dumbledore points out to Snape that Draco's soul is "not yet so damaged."[88] When it comes to it, he is "not a killer"[89] and lacks the heart to slay Dumbledore, despite the opportunity of "several long minutes" during which Dumbledore is defenseless.[90] By the end of the story he is on terms of acknowledgement with Harry, Ron, Hermione, and Ginny.[91]

Another possible opposition is that between Gryffindor and Slytherin houses. In this view, the battle between good and evil would be as simple as the Quidditch match between them in the first book.[92] This view is demolished in the first book itself, when the housemaster of Slytherin is revealed to have been giving Harry his protection during the same Quidditch match.[93] Even so, this notion of opposition perseveres to some extent in the minds of pupils of houses other than Slytherin. But the wisdom of the Sorting Hat's song about unity within Hogwarts—sung in Harry's fifth year[94]—is more than justified by the eventual extraordinary heroism of the housemaster of Slytherin.[95] It is also born out, to a lesser extent, by the streak of nobility in that other

Slytherin housemaster, Horace Slughorn, shown by his willingness to let Harry have the vital memory.[96] As Phineas Nigellus says, after the victory over Voldemort, "Let it be noted that Slytherin house played its part!"[97] And, in the end, Harry tells his own son, Albus, that it doesn't matter to him and his wife if their son is in Slytherin.[98]

No Perfect Embodiment

One final possible opposition between notional good and evil can be made. It is a simplification that costs Harry a great deal to get beyond. Indeed, it is only in the section of the series that deals with the struggle with evil in a relatively adult way—Books 5 to 7—that it begins to be questioned. That is the opposition between Dumbledore and Voldemort. Certainly, Dumbledore has important qualities that Voldemort has not. He trusts people, for example.[99] He recommends this quality to his students as a way of combating Voldemort: "Lord Voldemort's gift for spreading discord and enmity is very great. We can fight it only by showing an equally strong bond of friendship and trust."[100] Yet Dumbledore—great man, great wizard that he is—is shown to have feet of clay. In his youth, he is caught by the ideas of Grindelwald: "Muggles forced into subservience... wizards triumphant."[101] And in his age, he is "such a fool" that he picks up a cursed Horcrux in a vain attempt to make contact with the dead.[102]

In the end, the values that Harry needs are given to him by no single person or group. He learns that, as Sirius says, "The world isn't split into good people and Death Eaters."[103] He learns that the notions of good and evil that come most readily to mind are fallible.

His heroes are flawed, and those people he takes against are in some cases for him to the death: not only Snape, but also Lupin, with whom he is very angry,[104] and Scrimgeour. Harry refuses to do business with the latter, yet—it seems—Scrimgeour undergoes torture and death rather then betray him.[106] Harry finds that the question of good and evil is not a simple one. He is told of someone fighting evil who "became as ruthless and cruel as many on the Dark side."[107] At the age of fourteen, he learns of three curses that are considered to be "unforgivable."[108] Yet by the time he is eighteen, he himself has performed two of the three,[109] and the third curse—the Killing Curse—is performed by the mother of his best friend.[110] Harry is on a quest for what is good, in a world in which it is not evident in a pure form.

BRAVERY FOR THE BATTLE

Evil, however, is clearly manifest in Voldemort. And the need for it to be confronted makes obvious the foremost quality that Harry needs to fight him. The Sorting Hat spots at once that Harry has it. "Plenty of courage, I see," it says.[111] Without courage he could not fulfill his destiny: he could not be the hero of the series. Christian tradition tells us that fortitude is one of the four cardinal—that is, principal—virtues. Fortitude is close to being the same as courage; it emphasizes courage in endurance. We might say it is courage in a war rather than a battle. The Christian understanding of its necessity for right action is well brought out in Dumbledore's end-of-year speech in Book 4:

> "Remember Cedric. Remember, if the time should come when you have to make a choice between what is right, and what is easy, remember what

happened to a boy who was good, and kind, and brave, because he strayed across the path of Lord Voldemort. Remember Cedric Diggory."[112]

Fortitude is the habit of soul by which we *go on* doing what is right rather than what is easy. In its absence, evil gains sway and the "good, and kind, and brave"—like Cedric Diggory—are cut down by it.

If Christian tradition ultimately underpins this value of courage or fortitude in the series, the story also has its own tradition: that of Hogwarts. The Sorting Hat articulates this:

> *"You might belong in Gryffindor,*
> *Where dwell the brave at heart,*
> *Their daring nerve and chivalry*
> *Set Gryffindors apart."*[113]

Of course, people not in Gryffindor, like Cedric Diggory, can be brave. Indeed, as Harry points out to his young son, probably the bravest man he ever knew was a Slytherin.[114] Snape's bravery is extraordinary. He exposes himself to "constant danger" in order "to give Voldemort what appears to be valuable information while withholding the essentials."[115] He uses his closeness to Lord Voldemort to betray him. In order to keep his cover, he exposes himself to the opposition of all those against Lord Voldemort, and ends up "in full flight, McGonagall, Flitwick, and Sprout all thundering after him."[116] It is understandable that he should react with an expression of pain unusual for an accomplished Occlumens when Harry calls him a coward:

> "DON'T—" screamed Snape, and his face was suddenly demented, inhuman, as though he was in as much pain as the yelping, howling dog stuck

in the burning house behind them, "—CALL ME COWARD!"[117]

Snape is anything but a coward.

All the same, at Hogwarts, bravery remains associated with Gryffindor. In acknowledging Snape's bravery, Dumbledore says, "I sometimes think we Sort too soon."[118] Just as Harry has qualities that qualify him for Slytherin,[119] so Snape has qualities that qualify him for Gryffindor. Gryffindors are brave. Neville Longbottom is a notable example. Dumbledore commends him at the end of his first year at Hogwarts, saying, "There are all kinds of courage.... It takes a great deal of bravery to stand up to our enemies, but just as much to stand up to our friends."[120] Neville also has the bravery it takes to stand up to enemies. He shows bravery during torture during the fight in the Ministry of Magic in his fifth year.[121] He stands up to the evil Carrows at the cost of considerable personal injury.[122] In the face of Voldemort's threats in his seventh year, he says to Harry, "We're all going to keep fighting."[123] To Voldemort himself, when told he would be a very valuable Death Eater, he says, "I'll join you when hell freezes over."[124] He kills Nagini with the Sword of Gryffindor,[125] which lies by his plate as he eats (after it is all over), "surrounded by a knot of fervent admirers."[126] Ron is also a worthy wielder of the sword, recovering it from icy water and destroying a Horcrux with it.[127] It is he who breaks Voldemort's Silencing Charm by taunting him with what Harry has done, yelling, "He beat you!"[128]

Among the students, the greatest bravery is Harry's. "Harry Potter is valiant and bold!" says Dobby.[129] He wins Dumbledore's posthumous approval: "Harry, you wonderful boy. You brave, brave man," he says.[130] His mother gives a similar posthumous approval: "You've been so brave."[131] Professor McGonagall responds to Harry's chivalrous defense of her: "That was very—very *gallant* of you."[132] Perhaps empowered by the affirmation he receives, Harry is able to say to Voldemort's face: "I dare." He dares to correct Voldemort.[133] This ultimate in courage is the culmination of a whole series of courageous acts. In his first year at Hogwarts, with "outstanding courage,"[134] Harry bravely goes through the trapdoor to stop the Philosopher's Stone from falling into Voldemort's use.[135] In his second year, Gryffindor's Sword (to be "taken under conditions of need and valour")[136] is given to him, and with it he kills the Basilisk.[137] In his fourth year, he battles a Hungarian Horntail dragon and duels with Lord Voldemort.[138]

Harry inherits the Sword of Gryffindor.[139] He has learned what Dumbledore taught: that it is important to fight, and fight again, and keep fighting, for only then can evil be kept at bay, although never quite eradicated.[140] "We're fighting," Harry announces to his comrades. They rush into battle with "a great roar."[141] Kreacher later joins them, leading his fellow house-elves with the cry, "Fight! Fight!"[142] Harry is their inspiration, "a symbol," as Lupin says, "of everything for which we are fighting: the triumph of good, the power of innocence, the need to keep resisting."[143]

TRADITIONAL CHRISTIAN STRUGGLE

This emphasis on fighting evil, on continually resisting it, is very much part of the Christian tradition. For example, the early monk Saint Antony of the Desert embodies this ideal. His biography, written by Saint Athanasius, proposes him as a model of monastic and Christian virtue.[144] Saint Antony struggles with demons and goes out into the desert to take on the devil. Although his struggle is essentially an interior one, it corresponds to the struggle in the Harry

Potter series in that it is continual. Like Saint Antony, Harry and his friends have to keep resisting. Like Saint Antony, Harry's confrontation with evil demands that he be apart from people; he finds the solitude necessary for this confrontation by wearing the Invisibility Cloak.[145] Finally, Harry walks defenseless into the gathering of his mortal enemy.[146] He walks to face his death, true to his resolve: "I'm going to keep going until I succeed—or I die."[147]

Courage—fortitude—is not only about how the challenges of life are faced: it is also about how the challenge of death is faced, a challenge about which the Christian tradition has a lot to say. The next chapter looks at the series' teaching about life and death.

Notes

1. Mark 10:18.
2. *The Deathly Hallows*, 537.
3. *The Chamber of Secrets*, 133.
4. *The Deathly Hallows*, 357.
5. *The Deathly Hallows*, 512.
6. *The Goblet of Fire*, 366.
7. 2 Thessalonians 2:7 (King James Version).
8. *The Chamber of Secrets*, 231.
9. *Coriolanus*, act 5, scene 3, lines 36–37.
10. Mark 10:18.
11. John 1:11.
12. Luke 1:26–38.
13. *The Goblet of Fire*, 556.
14. *The Goblet of Fire*, 556–57.
15. *The Goblet of Fire*, 15.
16. *The Goblet of Fire*, 557.
17. *The Goblet of Fire*, 558.
18. 1 Corinthians 11:23–26.
19. *The Deathly Hallows*, 568.

20. Ezekiel 37:1–10.
21. Ezekiel 37:12 and 14.
22. *The Goblet of Fire*, 556.
23. John 1:1–2.
24. *The Goblet of Fire*, 556.
25. John 1:9.
26. *The Half-Blood Prince*, 26.
27. Matthew 28:18–19.
28. *The Deathly Hallows*, 596.
29. John 14:17 and 26.
30. *The Deathly Hallows*, 568.
31. Matthew 18:3.
32. *The Goblet of Fire*, 555–56.
33. *The Philosopher's Stone*, 160.
34. *The Philosopher's Stone*, 215.
35. Luke 9:24.
36. Genesis 3:1–7.
37. *The Goblet of Fire*, 532.
38. *The Deathly Hallows*, 281.
39. *The Deathly Hallows*, 444–45.
40. *The Deathly Hallows*, 577.
41. *The Half-Blood Prince*, 259–60.
42. *The Deathly Hallows*, 515.
43. Rule of Saint Benedict, chapter 7.
44. *The Half-Blood Prince*, 250–51.
45. Matthew 12:50.
46. John 19:27.
47. *The Deathly Hallows*, 234.
48. *The Order of the Phoenix*, 704.
49. *The Philosopher's Stone*, 148.
50. *The Chamber of Secrets*, 158.
51. *The Chamber of Secrets*, 159.
52. *The Prisoner of Azkaban*, 165.
53. *The Goblet of Fire*, chapter 23.

54. *The Order of the Phoenix*, chapter 23.
55. *The Half-Blood Prince*, chapter 16.
56. *The Deathly Hallows*, 265.
57. *The Deathly Hallows*, 279.
58. *The Deathly Hallows*, 591.
59. Matthew 2:16–18.
60. *The Philosopher's Stone*, 15.
61. Isaiah 53:5.
62. *The Deathly Hallows*, 444–46.
63. Philippians 2:6–7.
64. Philippians 2:7–8.
65. *The Deathly Hallows*, 556.
66. *The Deathly Hallows*, chapter 34.
67. *The Goblet of Fire*, 19.
68. *The Half-Blood Prince*, 465.
69. *The Half-Blood Prince*, 469.
70. *The Deathly Hallows*, 90.
71. *The Half-Blood Prince*, 465.
72. *The Half-Blood Prince*, 470.
73. *The Half-Blood Prince*, 469.
74. *The Half-Blood Prince*, 466.
75. *The Deathly Hallows*, 89.
76. Luke 11:9 (RSV).
77. *The Chamber of Secrets*, 86 and 89.
78. *The Goblet of Fire*, 108.
79. *The Deathly Hallows*, 199.
80. *The Chamber of Secrets*, 37.
81. *The Deathly Hallows*, 487.
82. *The Order of the Phoenix*, 41.
83. *The Deathly Hallows*, 39.
84. *The Philosopher's Stone*, 81.
85. *The Half-Blood Prince*, 35–36.
86. *The Chamber of Secrets*, 51.
87. *The Deathly Hallows*, 581.

88. *The Deathly Hallows*, 548.
89. *The Half-Blood Prince*, 546.
90. *The Half-Blood Prince*, 551.
91. *The Deathly Hallows*, 605.
92. *The Philosopher's Stone*, chapter 11.
93. *The Philosopher's Stone*, 209.
94. *The Order of the Phoenix*, 184–87.
95. *The Deathly Hallows*, 607.
96. *The Half-Blood Prince*, 459.
97. *The Deathly Hallows*, 598.
98. *The Deathly Hallows*, 607.
99. *The Goblet of Fire*, 395.
100. *The Goblet of Fire*, 627.
101. *The Deathly Hallows*, 573.
102. *The Deathly Hallows*, 576.
103. *The Order of the Phoenix*, 271.
104. *The Deathly Hallows*, 176.
105. *The Half-Blood Prince*, 323–26, and *The Deathly Hallows*, 110.
106. *The Deathly Hallows*, 169–70.
107. *The Goblet of Fire*, 457.
108. *The Goblet of Fire*, 192.
109. *The Deathly Hallows*, 428 and 477.
110. *The Deathly Hallows*, 589–90.
111. *The Philosopher's Stone*, 90.
112. *The Goblet of Fire*, 628.
113. *The Philosopher's Stone*, 88.
114. *The Deathly Hallows*, 607.
115. *The Deathly Hallows*, 549.
116. *The Deathly Hallows*, 482.
117. *The Half-Blood Prince*, 564.
118. *The Deathly Hallows*, 545.
119. *The Philosopher's Stone*, 91.
120. *The Philosopher's Stone*, 221.

121. *The Order of the Phoenix*, 706.

122. *The Deathly Hallows*, 462.

123. *The Deathly Hallows*, 558.

124. *The Deathly Hallows*, 586.

125. *The Deathly Hallows*, 587.

126. *The Deathly Hallows*, 597.

127. *The Deathly Hallows*, 302 and 307.

128. *The Deathly Hallows*, 585.

129. *The Chamber of Secrets*, 17.

130. *The Deathly Hallows*, 566.

131. *The Deathly Hallows*, 560.

132. *The Deathly Hallows*, 477.

133. *The Deathly Hallows*, 591–92.

134. *The Philosopher's Stone*, 221.

135. *The Philosopher's Stone*, 197.

136. *The Deathly Hallows*, 553.

137. *The Chamber of Secrets*, 235–36.

138. *The Goblet of Fire*, 309–11 and 575–80.

139. *The Deathly Hallows*, 109.

140. *The Half-Blood Prince*, 601.

141. *The Deathly Hallows*, 485.

142. *The Deathly Hallows*, 588.

143. *The Deathly Hallows*, 357–58.

144. *Athanasius: The Life of Antony and the Letter to Marcellinus*, translation and introduction by Robert C. Gregg, Classics of Western Spirituality (New York/Mahwah, NJ: Paulist Press, 1980).

145. *The Deathly Hallows*, 556.

146. *The Deathly Hallows*, 562–63.

147. *The Deathly Hallows*, 458.

4

Be Absolute for Death

LIFE AND DEATH

"See, I have set before you this day life and good, death and evil," says Moses in the Old Testament.[1] Life is linked with good, and death with evil. But good people die. People given over to evil kill good people. In examining JK's depiction of good and evil, we have seen that killing rips the soul apart. The life of the soul is more important than the life of the body. "If you're going to be cursed for ever, death's better, isn't it?"[2] says Harry at the age of eleven. That conviction deepens until, in a final showdown, Harry is able to confront Voldemort with his own shallowness.

We are given plenty of incentive not to murder. But evil, even though it is ultimately self-torturing in its practitioners, still happens, and it affects those who do not give themselves to it. Because of it, people die. This is the great fact that the Harry Potter series faces. It is about growing up and facing this. The death of Cedric Diggory is a turning point in the series, the point at which these books are not just for children: they are for children who are growing up.

Apparently, JK lost readers at this point. Some readers were happy with the children's outlook in the earlier books, in which death happened only to a bad character (Quirrell) and even then you didn't actually see it.[3] When the first death of a sympathetic person (Diggory) happened, they felt they had been let down.[4] This point—in the narrative is the rite of passage. Those who go beyond it become people who can see Thestrals. They are changed. When Sirius dies, Harry finds Luna strangely (for she *is* strange) sympathetic. She has seen her mother die; she can see Thestrals; she can comfort Harry.[5] This experience cannot be replaced by knowledge alone: Hermione, who knows all about Thestrals, tactlessly says to Harry that she wishes she could see them.[6] She has not faced death.

FACING UP TO DEATH

Facing death is a central theme of the series. Ultimately, this includes facing one's own death, as Harry faces "the incontrovertible truth...that he must die."[7] There are many ways of doing this and there lies the difference between good and evil. On the way to this, however, there are the deaths of others to be faced, and it makes sense to look at these first, because the way they are faced affects the way one's own death is faced.

Voldemort, as usual, has the least enlightened view of the matter. "My mother can't have been magic, or she wouldn't have died," he says as a boy.[8] This childish lack of acceptance of the limits of power (even magical power) is a more extreme denial of death than the repeated false hope that comes to Harry after the death of Sirius. Harry initially roars, "HE—IS—NOT—DEAD!"[9] He later tries to communicate with him through a two-way mirror.[10] He questions Nearly Headless Nick about the possibility of Sirius coming back in ghostly form, saying, "He'll come back, I know he will!"—only to be told, "He will not come back."[11]

Ron too gives way to the natural impulse to deny the reality of death, when he raises the possibility that it was Dumbledore who sent the Patronus in the Forest of Dean. Harry understands the longing behind Ron's question, but he answers, "Dumbledore's dead."[12] Again and again the denial of the reality of death is contradicted. "No spell can reawaken the dead,"[13] Dumbledore explains to Harry after Cedric's death. When Mad-Eye dies, Harry knows for himself "the suddenness and completeness of death," which is "with them like a presence."[14] This presence, which denial cannot keep at bay, is described in the first of the two quotations that preface the final book. It is from the Greek tragedian Aeschylus—by this point we have moved far from the chocolate-frog children's jollity of the first book—and describes eloquently the impact of death:

> Oh, the torment bred in the race,
>   the grinding scream of death
>   and the stroke that hits the vein,
>   the haemorrhage none can staunch, the grief,
> the curse no man can bear.[15]

This puts, in an adult way, the reality that Harry has been coming to terms with since the end of his fourth year, when Cedric Diggory dies. However, although it is only after this that he sees Thestrals, for Harry that reality is already deep in his consciousness from a much younger age: after all, he was there when Voldemort murdered his parents. At the beginning, the memory is inchoate and misinterpreted: "Sometimes, when he strained his memory during long hours in his cupboard, he came up with a strange vision: a blinding flash of green light and a burning pain on his forehead." Because he has been told that his parents died in a car crash, he interprets the memory as being about this.[16] He learns the truth about the way they died soon after,[17] but coming to terms with "the torment bred in the race"[18] is the work of his entire seven years at Hogwarts. Indeed, we may speculate that the whole series reflects the author's working out of her own experience of the early loss of her mother. She may be sifting her thoughts, as it were, in the "Pensieve of fiction."[19]

For Harry, the first fully aware sight of death is when he opens "his stinging eyes" to see Cedric "lying spread-eagled on the ground beside him."[20] Both the magnitude and the manner of the loss are carefully prepared in the narrative. We know Cedric is "extremely handsome"[21] and of generous disposition: he wants a rematch when Harry falls off his broom during a Quidditch game,[22] he congratulates Harry on getting his Firebolt,[23] and he shares the Triwizard Tournament clue he has with Harry.[24] There is a poignant reference to his grandchildren.[25] The capacity of a Portkey to sweep them from one place to another, and so into danger, has been illustrated when Harry and Cedric, among others, take the seven-past-five from Stoatshead Hill.[26] The impact of this first witnessed death takes Harry out of his normal experience of time: "For a second that contained an eternity Harry stared into Cedric's face, at his open grey eyes, blank and expressionless as the windows of a deserted house."[27] Harry's first reaction is "numb disbelief."[28] When he returns to Hogwarts, he is clinging tenaciously to Cedric's body.[29]

This first fully aware experience of death is, of course, only the start. In the book that follows, we have the first deeply upsetting death. The author herself wept at this one, and so did I. I read it on the Isles of Scilly, the most western point of the United Kingdom. Sitting on a folding chair off the main path around one of the tiny islands and looking, through tears, across to another, I absorbed the impact of the loss of Sirius. I was not alone. "We have to accept that we are living in a post-*Order of the Phoenix* world," wrote someone, who was also coming to terms with it, on a Web site devoted to Sirius Black. Why does this death make such an impact?

As Harry smashes up Dumbledore's personal possessions from the sheer pain of his love and loss, the pain of being human, the latter puts his finger on it. He says to Harry, "You have now lost your mother, your father, and the closest thing to a parent you have ever known."[30] It is the preciousness of the bond that makes this death so affecting. At its first forming, "Some sort of explosion took place in the pit of Harry's stomach."[31] The moment is no less transformative for Sirius. In his loss, Harry remembers how Sirius looked when his "gaunt face broke into the first true smile Harry had seen upon it. The difference it made was startling, as though a person ten years younger was shining through the starved mask; for a moment, he was recognizable as the man who had laughed at Harry's parents' wedding."[32] The movie of the third book deals with this bonding too fast to show its true depth, but the book retains its power to communicate it.

The death of Sirius is deeply affecting for readers because the depth of Harry's bond with him reflects the importance of this sort of bond in everybody's life, whether from the point of view of the younger or the older. It is particularly affecting because, as Dumbledore implies, it is in effect a double loss. Harry loses his parents and, in a sense, finds them again in their appointed representative, his godparent and guardian,[33] so when he loses Sirius, it is also a loss of his parents, and this for the second time. The hope that he has invested in this bond is a hope that has fought against a loss sustained when he was only one year old. The agony and anger that he feels when his hope is (subjectively) betrayed for the second time is natural. He is cut off from his origins. That agony and anger is a reflection of all "the torment bred in the race"[34]—the severing, through death, of the links with our origin.

This universal theme is powerfully presented by another contemporary novelist, Kazuo Ishiguro, in *When We Were Orphans*. The main character of this novel spends his life pursuing the memory of the father who abandoned him, only to be disappointed by the reality he uncovers. Aeschylus, JK, and Ishiguro are all writing of the same thing: the pain of the loss of connection with our origins. Ultimately, this is the pain of the loss of connection with God, our first origin. Harry's struggle to cope with the fact of death is ultimately a struggle to find his own connection with God as he loses the obscurely mediated connection that comes to him through his parents and others who have a similar role.

Dumbledore's Death

If Sirius represents Harry's link with his origins, mediating his link with God—ultimate origin and author of all—then so does Dumbledore. It is not simply that Dumbledore knew his parents and made arrangements for Harry's future when he was orphaned.[35] Dumbledore has authority in a way that is connected to the sense of origin and author. He has the authority of Headmaster. This is a true authority that commands respect. For all his eccentricity, he is freely acknowledged to be "the best wizard in the world."[36] His astonishing power as a wizard, which we later learn is connected with his holding of the Elder Wand, gives him an almost effortless supremacy—as Cornelius Fudge, Minister of Magic, discovers to his cost when he tries to have him arrested.[37] Dumbledore's given name, Albus, means "white" in Latin and speaks of innocence and goodness.

The same day that Hagrid tells Harry he is a wizard, he also says approvingly, "Great man, Dumbledore."[38] This is only the first of many expressions of approval and respect for Dumbledore from many quarters. Given his power, his apparent goodness, and the breadth of the respect that he enjoys as Headmaster of Hogwarts, it is not too much to say that for Harry, in his early years at school, Dumbledore represents God. Indeed, he recalls to my mind a particularly distinguished Benedictine headmaster, whose nickname was, simply, "God."

Dumbledore does not, of course, have the omnipotence, the omniscience, or the goodness of God, and Harry's gradual discovery that this is so is part of his own search for the good and the true, the development of his own values, and so, ultimately, of his own quest for God. Some of the questions that are raised for Harry about Dumbledore come after his death. The death itself, though, takes away a presence through which values—and hence, obscurely, God—are mediated. For Harry, his death is very different from that of Sirius. That was a private grief, which could be communicated only to the few who understood that the public view of Sirius was mistaken. The many, who do not know the truth about him, are unable to share it. Dumbledore's death affects everyone. It is a public grief. All are affected by "the enormous and incomprehensible truth" that Dumbledore can no longer help them. His wisdom, the fact that he is "the greatest wizard...ever," and the fact that he is the one whose leadership and guidance make witches and wizards what they are: all this makes his breaking the shattering of a whole society.[39]

Everybody dresses their best for the funeral. Hagrid, Ginny, Hermione, Harry, and Ron weep. Without him, the school becomes "not really like Hogwarts any more."[40] The death of Dumbledore is nonetheless a very particular grief for Harry: he is unprepared for seeing him "spread-eagled, broken."[41] Its manner also raises a question for the reader: if, from a Christian point of view, we say that Dumbledore's choice of death ignores the spiritual possibilities of a life that includes suffering,[42] we can also say that the story encourages us to see that even great teachers, like Dumbledore, have their weaknesses and can be wrong.

Deaths in "Deathly Hallows"

In the final volume of the series, there is a crescendo in "the grinding scream of death."[43] Each of the multiple losses is shocking in its own way. Both the sweet and the tough are lost. Hedwig, reminder and messenger of Harry's links with the magical world during his captivity at 4 Privet Drive— "the only living creature in this house who didn't flinch at the sight of him,"[44] is the first to be hit.[45] This slaughter of the innocent is immediately followed by the death of Mad-Eye Moody,[46] "so tough, so brave, the consummate survivor."[47] This loss of one so safety-conscious signals the reign of danger. Dobby's death, uttering Harry's name in a final expression of loyalty, is a cruel culmination of injustice.[48]

Perhaps the greatest pathos in this last novel, however, attaches to the death of Fred. It is carefully prepared in the course of the series. His mother weeps at the thought that he might have died in the trouble at the World Quidditch Cup, with her last words to him having been shouted.[49] Fred jokes shortly afterward that he and his twin might die in a train crash, with her last words "an unfounded accusation."[50]

He jokingly talks of his own wedding.[51] Poignantly, shortly before he dies, he holds out his hand to Percy in a gesture of reconciliation for the whole Weasley family.[52] And when it comes, his death follows immediately the sharing of a joke with Percy,[53] just as his first words in the series were a joke.[54] It seems that after the death of innocence, safety, and justice comes the death of laughter.

Fred's death engages the reader because he is well known, but he is only one of many who die in the final conflict with Voldemort. As well as Fred, with whom we laughed, there is Colin Creevey, *at* whom we perhaps laughed. A milkman's son, whom Harry once told angrily to get out of the way,[55] Colin is on the margins of the story. He has always been devoted to Harry, and there is pathos in his being "tiny in death."[56] There is Lupin, on whom Harry has been hard,[57] and Tonks, who once rescued him from going back to London on the same train as he came on.[58] Along with their bodies are the bodies of "fifty others who had died fighting." Their bodies are separated from the body of Voldemort, who dies outside human fellowship.[59]

In death there is division. Yet the dividing line is not always obvious. When Snape is dying, Harry does not know why he is approaching him, or what he feels.[60] There is a truth hidden from him, though he acts on it. Spiritually, Snape is a Gryffindor, a wizard of enormous courage.[61] And there is, finally, communion between him and Harry. His whispered dying words to Harry are, "Look…at…me…"[62] In Harry's green eyes, Snape sees again the eyes of Lily, whom he loves. Finally, for a second, he connects with the boy he hated because of his father, and understands what Dumbledore has already told him, that Harry's "deepest nature is much more like his mother's."[63]

Serenity in the Face of Death

Snape dies a hero's death. He does not swerve from his mission through fear. Fear of death is natural, but it does not have to be in control. When it is, life is diminished. Nearly Headless Nick confesses, "I was afraid of death....I chose to remain behind."[64] As a result, he becomes the ghost of his former self. Fear of death, of course, relates to fear of others' death as well as one's own. Such fear hangs over the Order of the Phoenix. Harry finds a photograph of the original order to be disturbing when he reflects on how many have died or gone mad.[65] Mrs. Weasley's fear of the death of her nearest and dearest, about which she dreams all the time, is manifest in a Boggart. This vanishes in a puff of smoke when Lupin says, very firmly and clearly, "*Riddikulus!*"[66] Laughter vanquishes fear.

Fred Weasley is the poster boy for this. When, during the night following a party, the house is awakened by a terrified scream and people come down to the common room, Fred says brightly, "Excellent, are we carrying on?"[67] As the Hogwarts castle quakes with the tremor of the deadly battle taking place there, he shouts, "Nice night for it!"[68] To him, the battle is "the fun."[69] The uncertainty does not worry him. When he is told that there is no plan, he responds, "Just going to make it up as we go along, are we? My favorite kind."[70] His whole approach is summarized in his attitude to the Triwizard tournament: "Where's the fun without a bit of risk?"[71] Fred dies, but he has lived intensely. His death realizes one of Mrs. Weasley's fears, but Fred also takes *away* one of her fears just before he dies. In being the Weasley who offers the hand of reconciliation to Percy, Fred makes sure it does not come to pass that something dreadful happens and they haven't made it up with him, as she fears.[72] In the end, the love in the family is not broken. Fred dies, his values do not.

In his laughter, in his bravery, Fred overcomes death, even as he succumbs to it. Like Ignotus in Beedle the Bard's "Tale of the Three Brothers," Fred goes with death gladly.[73] He is one of several characters in the series who model a serene acceptance of death. Nicolas Flamel is introduced on the back of a chocolate-frog card on the first journey to Hogwarts.[74] Hermione's researches in the library reveal that he owns the only Philosopher's Stone in existence, which explains why he still enjoys a quiet life with his wife in Devon at the age of six hundred and sixty-five.[75] He and his wife agree to the stone's destruction, as being "all for the best," though it means "they will die." Dumbledore explains, "To Nicholas and Perenelle, it really is like going to bed after a very, *very* long day. After all, to the well-organized mind, death is but the next great adventure."

This willingness to die amazes the young Harry, yet before he is eighteen he has learned it himself. He also learns about the value of renunciation. Dumbledore tells him that the Philosopher's Stone is "really not such an amazing thing" because "as much money and life as you could want," although widely desired, is harmful.[76] At the end of the series, Harry makes the "wise and courageous decision" not to go looking for the Resurrection Stone that he dropped in the forest.[77] He also willingly renounces the use of the Elder Wand. His forswearing of the power of command is redolent of the vows that monks and nuns take to be obedient. Harry is going further than his teacher in dying to the world.

Nonetheless, Dumbledore is his greatest exemplar of a serene and joyful freedom of fear of death. He is terminally ill from the curse injury to his hand, yet on his visit to the Dursleys to collect Harry for his sixth year at Hogwarts, he is smiling and cheerful.[78] When he stands to make his beginning-of-term speech and whispers sweep the Great Hall at the sight of his cursed hand, he says airily, "Nothing to worry about."[79] The sight of dead men does not trouble him. When Harry reacts to the sight of the Inferi, he says, "There is nothing to be feared from a body, Harry, any more than there is anything to be feared from the darkness....It is the unknown we fear when we look upon death and darkness, nothing more."[80] To Dumbledore, death is an allure of "that flighty temptress, adventure."[81] He asks conversationally how long he has to live, and smiles when he is told it is less than a year, as though it were "a matter of little of no concern to him."[82] Indeed, he welcomes the news, as giving him an opportunity to exercise spiritual care of the young Malfoy.[83]

Harry learns acceptance and mastery of death at Hogwarts. He is a promising pupil. Already in his first year, he prefers death to going over to the Dark Side.[84] Avoiding death is never an absolute for him, as it is for Voldemort. In his fifth year at Hogwarts, when he is being used by Voldemort to entice Dumbledore to kill him, Harry thinks, "Let him kill us....Death is nothing compared to this." In the extremity of his distress he glimpses the hope of something beyond death, thinking, "And I'll see Sirius again."[85] It is in his final year, however, that he realizes fully his destiny as "the true master of Death."[86] He does this by standing and facing death.[87] "The true master does not seek to run away from Death. He accepts that he must die, and understands that there are far, far worse things in the living world than dying."[88] Harry accepts the destiny of "the true master." He knows his job is "to walk calmly into Death's welcoming arms."[89] As the Book of Revelation says: "Whoever conquers will not be harmed by the second death."[90] Unlike Voldemort's, Harry's life beyond this life is not at risk. In the ante-chamber of eternity (King's

Cross), Dumbledore tells him, "You have less to fear from returning here than he does."[91]

This is the result of the choices that Harry makes. In the "Tale of the Three Brothers," which is, on one level, "a story about how humans are frightened of death,"[92] he is presented with the possibility of finding "three objects, or Hallows, which, if united, will make the possessor master of Death."[93] He turns this over in his mind and imagines himself triumphing over Voldemort through it.[94] But he comes to understand that this is a false trail: when he has to decide whether to pursue the Hallows, or stick fast to his destined task of destroying the Horcruxes that enable Voldemort's survival, he makes the decision to be true to his destiny, to pursue the Horcruxes.[95]

HARRY'S WILLINGNESS TO LOSE HIS LIFE

In the spirit of the gospel teaching,[96] Harry abandons the life seemingly offered him by the Hallows to find his true life in sacrifice to defeat evil, both in the Horcruxes and in the person of Lord Voldemort. In fact, as noted above, the Hallows do enable him to be master of death, in the sense of not letting the prospect of apparently certain death intimidate him into failing to carry out his heroic task of confronting Voldemort. Unselfishly seeking the good of others, Harry finds that the Hallows are there for him. Harry catches the final Hallow, the Elder Wand, "with the unerring skill of the Seeker."[97] He seeks the true good, and so, as the gospel promises, he finds.[98]

This final finding echoes his seeing the Philosopher's Stone in the mirror of Erised, which reflects the true quest of his heart.[99] This stone, found in his first year, anticipates the stone he finds "at the close." It is when he whispers, "I am about to die," that the Snitch breaks open to reveal the Resurrection Stone.[100] His willingness to die breaks the barrier of death, and those he has loved and lost are there for him "neither ghost nor truly flesh." As saints invoked at the litany of the dying, these ghosts give him courage. They are "fetching him," so that he may join them.[101] It is in holiness—that is, heroic sacrifice for good—that Harry finds the Hallows. The Hallows enable and confirm the sacrifice, the holiness. They hallow; that is, they make holy.

Harry becomes like the youngest in the "Tale of the Three Brothers," the one who does not trust the promises of death. The brother wisely chooses the Invisibility Cloak to escape[102] and returns to meet death only later, when he is ready. Harry too meets death on equal terms.[103] He uses the Invisibility Cloak to walk into Voldemort's forest camp, where he fully expects to be killed.[104] It is, however, Voldemort, the source of death, who consequently dies.

Beedle's tale and Voldemort's doom echo one of the only two direct quotations from scripture in the Potter books: "*The last enemy that shall be destroyed is death.*"[105] In Beedle's "Tale of the Three Brothers," the youngest, thanks to his earlier escape by invisibility, takes death with him when he goes of his own will ("equals, they departed this life").[106] By his willingness to die, Harry, also under a Cloak of Invisibility, abolishes the reign of the One Who Wants Death. Both of these point to the series' reflection of the fundamental Christian narrative: that Christ, his divinity hidden under the cloak of his humanity, destroys the sovereignty of death by his willing death on the cross. Harry's struggle with death is not like Voldemort's creation of Horcruxes; it is not even like Dumbledore's quest "to conquer death"[107] through the quest for the Hallows. Harry's struggle successfully ends Voldemort's sway because, as Dumbledore tells him, he accepts, even embraces, the possibility of death.[108] Harry goes with death gladly.

RESURRECTION

And at the end he finds himself alive.

The Harry Potter series is not only about death, it is also about resurrection. This is signaled in the second quotation that prefaces the last book. The first (from Aeschylus) is about the pain of the death; the second (from William Penn) is about the comfort that, in God, friends live beyond death:

> Death is but crossing the world, as friends do the seas; they live in one another still. For they must needs be present, that love and live in that which is omnipresent. In this divine glass they see face to face.[109]

The phrase *face to face* is an echo of Saint Paul's First Letter to the Corinthians, in which he compares this life to the next, saying: "For now we see in a mirror, dimly, but then we will see face to face."[110] For Christians, the resurrection of Christ is the pledge of life beyond death for those who follow him. As Saint Paul writes later in the same letter, "In fact Christ has been raised from the dead, the first fruits of those who have died."[111]

The traditional and natural symbol for Christ's resurrection is the dawn, when night gives way to light. It recalls not only the words of Saint John—"The light shines in the darkness, and the darkness did not overcome it"[112] — but also the account of the resurrection in Saint Matthew's Gospel, in which, "as the first day of the week was dawning," Mary Magdalene and the other Mary go to the tomb of Jesus and encounter an angel who tells them, "He is not here; for he has been raised."[113] This symbol is used to mark the significance of the final showdown between Harry and Voldemort, in which Voldemort and his Death Eaters are defeated, the reign of death is ended, and Harry lives. Harry announces that he is "the true master of the Elder Wand," and this passage immediately follows:

> A red-gold glow burst suddenly across the enchanted sky above them, as an edge of dazzling sun appeared over the sill of the nearest window. The light hit both of their faces at the same time, so that Voldemort's was suddenly a flaming blur. Harry heard the high voice shriek as he, too, yelled his best hope to the heavens, pointing Draco's wand:
> "*Avada Kedavra!*"
> "*Expelliarmus!*"[114]

Harry's spell is yelled "to the heavens." It is in effect a prayer. It is answered. The light shines in the darkness and the darkness does not overcome it.[115] The Elder Wand, which is Voldemort's power, flies high, "dark against the sunrise."[116] The dawn has come. The resurrection defeats the powers of death. The narrative records: "The sun rose steadily over Hogwarts, and the Great Hall blazed with life and light."[117] Light symbolizes life: they belong together. The sun rises, as Christ rises, bringing life to all.

The whole idea of the resurrection has been carefully prepared in the series. In the second book the Petrified Hermione is gripping a page of an ancient text. It says, "The Basilisk has a murderous stare, and all who are fixed with the beam of its eye shall suffer instant death." The Basilisk is, in effect, the presence of death. There is only one way to drive it away: "The Basilisk flees only from the crowing of the rooster, which is fatal to it."[118] The rooster represents dawn, symbol of the resurrection. This traditional association is made in Shakespeare's *Hamlet*:

> Some say that ever 'gainst that season comes
> Wherein our Saviour's birth is celebrated,
> This bird of dawning singeth all night long,
> And then they say no spirit dare stir abroad,
> The nights are wholesome, then no planets strike,
> No fairy takes, nor witch hath power to charm,
> So hallowed, and so gracious, is that time.[119]

The "bird of dawning," associated with Christ, who rises from the dead, and Christmas night, when his birth is celebrated, is said to be marked by its constant singing. This precludes evil. However, the Basilisk in the Chamber of Secrets lives on, because Hagrid's roosters have been killed.[120] Ginny Weasley is taken "right into the Chamber itself."[121] If the rising of the sun as Voldemort is killed is the herald of the light and life of Easter, then the setting of the sun on the day that Ginny is taken is the darkness of Good Friday. Harry sees "the sun sinking, blood-red, below the skyline." It is the worst he has ever felt.[122] Light has gone from him, and, though he does not know it explicitly, so has his life gone: it is the future mother of his children who is held captive. There are no roosters to crow the dawn.

However, there is another bird that represents the resurrection: Fawkes, the phoenix. As Dumbledore explains to Harry, "Phoenixes burst into flame when it is time for them to die and are reborn from the ashes." Harry sees this happen to Fawkes. Before the burning, he is "a decrepit-looking bird" resembling "a half-plucked turkey."[123] This recalls the

BAPTIZING Harry Potter

Suffering Servant prophecy traditionally applied to the One who died on Good Friday: "He had no form or majesty that we should look at him, nothing in his appearance that we should desire him."[124] Like the glory of the Lord, Fawkes's true beauty is veiled as he dies. "He's really very handsome most of the time: wonderful red and gold plumage."[125] Fawkes is the image of the Lord of Life. The Lord "has borne our infirmities and carried our iniquities;"[126] Phoenixes "can carry immensely heavy loads."[127] "By his bruises we are healed;"[128] the tears of phoenixes "have healing powers."[129] Harry wonders what chance a phoenix has against the king of serpents,[130] but Fawkes defeats the one "more crafty than any other wild animal,"[131] as the Lord of Life undoes the result of the serpent's temptation, which "brought death into the world, and all our woe":[132]

> Fawkes dived. His long golden beak sank out of sight and a sudden shower of dark blood spattered the floor. The snake's tail thrashed, narrowly missing Harry, and before Harry could shut his eyes, it turned. Harry looked straight into its face, and saw that its eyes, both its great bulbous yellow eyes, had been punctured by the phoenix: blood was streaming to the floor and the snake was spitting in agony.[133]

Harry looks directly into the yellow and death-dealing eyes, but he does not die because the bird of resurrection has punctured them. This anticipates the pupils of Voldemort's eyes contracting to thin slits when Harry confronts him with the truth about what he has done and suggests he tries for some remorse.[134] Again, it is not Harry who dies. As it is the Basilisk that dies,[135] so it is Voldemort, "the slit pupils of the scarlet eyes rolling upwards."[136]

Eyes

The color of the eyes is significant. Like the yellow eyes of the Basilisk, the red eyes of Voldemort are unnatural. Both signify danger and death. Nagini, another death-dealing serpent, also has unnaturally colored eyes: they are milky.[137] By contrast, the characters that are on the side of life have naturally colored eyes. Harry's are bright green,[138] like his mother's, as he is told first by Ollivander in his shop,[139] and then so often he finds it a bit wearing.[140] Just before his encounter with Voldemort in the forest, "her green eyes, so like his" give him a life-dealing look.[141] Green is the color of life. *Sancta viriditas* ("Holy greenness"), sang Saint Hildegard. Green is for good, green is for going from generation to generation: Albus Potter too has green eyes.[142] James Potter's are hazel.[143] Both Ron and Dumbledore have blue eyes.[144] Blue is the color of innocence, of the sky, of heaven. Ron's engagingly boyish naivety, which tends to lead him to say what he is thinking and feeling rather than what is tactful, is a sort of innocence. Dumbledore's innocence—hard-won, as we later learn—is indicated by his first name, Albus, meaning "white" in Latin.

The word *alb* is still used in the Church to indicate the white garment worn by the newly baptized as a sign of innocence. Dumbledore's eyes remain piercingly blue, except when they turn green in the reflected light of the basin in the cave that holds the locket.[145] Ron's, however, are at one pointed tainted by Voldemort's color when he is tempted to undervalue himself. When he is being influenced by the Horcrux that he is trying to destroy, there is, Harry thinks, "a trace of scarlet in his eyes."[146] If there is momentary ambiguity about Ron, it is quite clear that Narcissa Malfoy is not simply identified with the Death Eaters. Her eyes are blue too, and they are filled with tears as she thinks of her son, Draco.[147] In the end, she is on the side of life. She tells Voldemort that Harry is dead, and so stops an assault on Hogwarts in which her son would have been at risk.[148] Mrs. Weasley's eyes are "precisely the same shade of brown as Ginny's."[149] They are mothers both, imaged by the brown fecundity of earth, source of the green of new life. Grawp's eyes are sludge-colored:[150] he is on the side of life too, though maybe not in a very controlled way.

The eyes of Snape, an accomplished Occlumens, are "fathomless black,"[151] like "dark tunnels."[152] Black is the color of mystery. As Snape fixes his black eyes upon "Narcissa's tear-filled blue ones,"[153] she does not know if he is on the side of Lord Voldemort or her son Draco. The truth, which she does not imagine, is that he is on her son's side, but not Voldemort's. Harry's many encounters with Snape do not uncover his mystery. It is only after the green eyes find the black for the last time, and Snape dies,[154] that Harry discovers the truth.[155] In that final encounter is the mystery of life and death. Goblins too are mysterious and unfathomable. Griphook's eyes are black.[156] Lucius Malfoy's are gray.[157] Perhaps that indicates his suffering: Cedric Diggory's eyes are gray too.[158]

It is as though the characters are color-coded through their eyes. Often significant moments in the narrative are marked by the meeting of eyes. The mystery of suffering and hope is in them—the tension between the agony of loss through death, as described by Aeschylus, and the conviction of reunion through God, as described by William Penn.[159] This latter hope, as we have seen, is imaged by Fawkes, bird of the resurrection. Not only does he puncture the eyes of the Basilisk, but his tears heal the wound on Harry's arm caused by the Basilisk fang.[160]

Healing Sacrifice

In Christian tradition and belief, the death and resurrection of Christ have power to heal as well as to overcome death. This is healing from the sin brought into the world by the temptation of the serpent,[161] and also, as and when God wills, healing of the body. Through the sacrifice of Christ, those who trust in him can reach heaven; Harry and his friends reach out to hold onto Fawkes, and he finds an extraordinary lightness spreading through his body. The next second they are flying upward, escaping from the dark Chamber.[162] This is the realization of the intuition that Harry has when he first hears the phoenix song. It is "unearthly" and makes his heart feel as though it is swelling to twice its normal size.[163]

The next time he hears it, it is clear why it makes his heart swell: the sound brings hope. He hears it during his duel with Voldemort in the graveyard after their wands are connected by a "thread of shimmering golden light":[164]

> And then an unearthly and beautiful sound filled the air....It was coming from every thread of the light-spun web vibrating around Harry and Voldemort. It was a sound Harry recognized, though he had heard it only once before in his life...phoenix song...
>
> It was the sound of hope to Harry...the most beautiful and welcome thing he had ever heard in his life.[165]

The song is "unearthly" because it sings of the life of the resurrection; it is "beautiful" because that life has a celestial beauty beyond anything on this earth; "it is the sound of hope" because it announces that death is not the last word—there is something beyond. In the context of the duel with the incarnation of the One Who Wants Death—for others, Voldemort thinks, but in the deeper reality, since he cuts himself off from the beauty that is beyond, for himself—the sound is particularly "welcome." The music seems to speak to Harry, telling him what to do,[166] and he struggles with Voldemort, "his ears full of phoenix song."[167]

Although, as Dumbledore later tells Harry, "no spell can reawaken the dead,"[168] what follows is an indication of "things in heaven and earth"[169] that are beyond what can be seen, an intimation of immortality: the forms of those whom Voldemort has murdered with his wand emerge from it.[170] The connected wands speak of the resurrection: they both have in them a feather from the bird of resurrection, Fawkes, the phoenix.[171] Fawkes is with Harry as he talks through with Dumbledore the horror of what happened in the graveyard, and the bird's "thick pearly tears" once more bring healing:[172] this time, of the wound inflicted on him by the spider in the maze.[173] And once more Fawkes is a means of escape, as he was in the Chamber: Dumbledore escapes holding "the phoenix's long golden tail" when Fudge tries to have him apprehended.[174] He also literally saves Dumbledore from death, swallowing a Death Curse directed at him.[175] But it is not his end. He is the bird of the resurrection, and he becomes again a baby, making "soft chirruping noises in his nest of ashes."[176]

Hints of Heaven

The presence of Fawkes is a reminder that "this muddy vesture of decay" does not define the limits of our life.[177] His song communicates the hope of the resurrection. When Dumbledore does die, Fawkes sings "a stricken lament of terrible beauty.''[178] It is stricken and terrible because the hope it represents does not take away the grief of loss of which Aeschylus wrote; it is beautiful because it brings the hope of which William Penn wrote.[179] There is another possible interpretation of the beauty. It could be the beauty of the art that takes the terrible fact of death and makes of it something of aesthetic beauty. It could be argued that the whole Harry Potter series is such an artistic rendering of the awful fact of death.

Yet art at its highest—and I believe that JK does reach this height—is informed with something beyond this world, something of heaven. It communicates what is unseen through what is seen, what cannot be said through what can be said. The grief that becomes song intimates the transformation of tribulation into bliss at the end of time. Yet the intuition that there is some special gift of grace in each sorrow is not one that is sensibly felt at all times. The greatest saints have known periods when there have been a total absence of the sense of heaven and no feeling of resurrection as a reality. This dark night of the spirit is the purification of the soul, so that it becomes totally disinterested in its love for God, not even enjoying any feeling of it. Harry undergoes something that speaks of this:

> He became aware suddenly that the grounds were silent. Fawkes had stopped singing.
> And he knew, without knowing how he knew it, that the phoenix had gone, had left Hogwarts for good, just as Dumbledore had left the school, had left the world…had left Harry.[180]

Harry knows the desolation of being alone, without any feeling of what is beyond.

GATHERING OF BELIEVERS

Yet he is never entirely alone. The phoenix, the bird of resurrection, does not belong to him alone. There are others who have heard its secret, who know that death is not the worst thing that can happen to a person. There are others who fight against the sick empire of Voldemort, who uses the death of others to try to protect himself from ever dying. And these people were around long before Harry came to know about Voldemort. They form the Order of the Phoenix. Hermione explains what it is toward the beginning of the fifth book: "It's a secret society....Dumbledore's in charge, he founded it. It's the people who fought against You-Know-Who last time."[181] If we can compare Harry's hearing of the phoenix song to the individual believer coming to faith in the resurrection, then the Order of the Phoenix can be compared to the Church. The Church is the gathering of those who believe in the resurrection, who believe that death is not the worst that can happen to a person, contrary to Voldemort's claim that "there is nothing worse than death."[182] Each is committed to the struggle against evil. Like the Order of the Phoenix, which has the experience of the earlier struggle against Voldemort, the Church has a wisdom and a tradition that comes from the struggles of its history.

The Order is an organization that is committed to behaving in a way that assumes that death is not the worst that can happen to a person. It implies a belief in what is beyond. There are also individuals who bear witness to such a belief. One of these is Luna Lovegood. Harry's dialogue with her is the series' first clear intimation of life after death. She speaks of it confidently:

> "And anyway, it's not as though I'll never see Mum again, is it?"

"Er—isn't it?" said Harry uncertainly.

She shook her head in disbelief.

"Oh, come on. You heard them, just behind the veil, didn't you?"

"You mean…"

"In that room with the archway. They were just lurking out of sight, that's all. You heard them."

They looked at each other. Luna was smiling slightly. Harry did not know what to say, or to think; Luna believed so many extraordinary things…yet he had been sure he had heard voices behind the veil, too.[183]

Luna's allusion to the archway relates to Harry's experience in the Ministry of Magic. The archway there is described as "hung with a tattered black curtain or veil which, despite the complete stillness of the cold surrounding air was fluttering very slightly as though it had just been touched." Harry has the strangest feeling that there is someone standing right behind the veil on the other side of the archway. He hears "faint whispering, murmuring noises coming from the other side of the veil." Luna is clear about the meaning of this: "There are people *in there*!" she says.[184] This is the veil through which (literally) Sirius Black passes,[185] and Luna's reminding Harry of his experience brings him the beginning of hope that, as with Luna and her mother, he will one day see Sirius again.

LIFE AFTER DEATH

The Harry Potter series is like the Bible in that it only gradually introduces the idea of life after death. To begin with, there are only uncertain intimations, such as Luna's testimony (which is somewhat clouded by her equal willingness to believe in such things as the Crumple-Horned Snorkack)[186] and Nearly Headless Nick's admission that, while he knows nothing of the secrets of death, he believes "learned wizards study the matter in the Department of Mysteries."[187] It is not until the final book that more explicit testimony is introduced. First of all, there is the testimony of scripture itself. On the tomb of Dumbledore's mother and sister is written the second of the only two direct quotations in the whole series: "Where your treasure is, there will your heart be also."[188] This is from Saint Matthew's Gospel;[189] the immediately preceding verse makes clear its context:

> "But lay up for yourselves treasures in heaven, where neither moth nor rust doth corrupt, and where thieves do not break through nor steal."[190]

As a tombstone inscription, the quotation points to the heavenly reward that is hoped for for the ones who are buried there. As a text relating to the whole Harry Potter series, it is saying that there is life after death, but its implications go beyond this. It refers to the brave members of the Order of the Phoenix, past and present, and Harry and his friends, all of whom, at least by their actions, show that their hearts are not locked upon the things of this world. They trust in what is beyond, and so have free hearts. Unlike Voldemort, who feels he has to avoid his own death, however terrible the consequences of this approach, they can risk their own lives in the service of noble values.

The other direct quotation from scripture, cited above, also indicates that death does not have the final power to control human actions. It is on the white marble tomb of Harry's parents and says, "The last enemy that shall be destroyed is death."[191] This is about the victory of Christ over death. It follows on from the statement "in Christ shall all be made alive,"[192] and the announcement of "the end…when he shall have put down all rulers and all authority and power."[193] If all are made alive in Christ, and if at the end he puts down all rule, authority, and power, then we have no need to fear the power of evil to kill us. That power will come to an end, and we shall live. So this quotation from the Bible is very relevant to the Order of the Phoenix.

James and Lily Potter have not been wiped definitively out of existence, while Lord Voldemort's power will come to an end. He cannot really win, in the end. The same sort of point about the immortality of the soul is made by Hermione before the friends leave the Burrow in the final book: "Look, if I picked up a sword right now, Ron, and ran you through with it, I wouldn't damage your soul at all."[194] It follows from this that Lord Voldemort cannot control people by the threat of death, providing that they are confident at some level that this is so. For the man or woman of faith, death is not a compelling threat.

However, the series does more than depict faith in life beyond death. It depicts *life beyond death* itself, in the chapter entitled "King's Cross."[195] The title comes from the answer that Harry gives when Dumbledore asks where they are: "It looks like King's Cross station. Except a lot cleaner, and empty, and there are no trains as far as I can see." Dumbledore says that he himself has no idea where they are, telling Harry, "This is, as they say, *your* party."[196] This implies that it is, as it were, a celebration for Harry. It is his heaven. *Party* evokes the eschatological banquet; that is, heaven, understood as a feast following the final judgment, as evoked by the prophet Isaiah:

> On this mountain the LORD of hosts will make for all peoples

a feast of rich food, a feast of well-aged wines,
of rich food filled with marrow, of well-aged wines
   strained clear.
And he will destroy on this mountain
   the shroud that is cast over all peoples,
   the sheet that is spread over all nations;
   he will swallow up death for ever.[197]

TIME AND ETERNITY

This is the destruction of death that the Bible quotation on the tomb of Harry's parents speaks of.[198] After death's destruction, there is only celebration. It is highly significant that it should look like King's Cross station to Harry. King's Cross is where his magical adventure began.[199] In one sense, Harry is already living beyond this life when he boards the Hogwarts Express. His entire magical experience can be seen as belonging to another world, and it is a world he gets to by the Hogwarts Express. When Dumbledore explains to Harry that he has a choice about whether to go back (to his earthly life) or not, he says, "We are in King's Cross, you say? I think that if you decided not to go back, you would be able to...let's say...board a train." He replies to the question, "And where would it take me?" with a simple word, "On."[200] The Hogwarts Express in the first instance takes him "on"—he has the embarrassing experience of not being able to tell the guard at King's Cross "what part of the country" Hogwarts is in.[201]

When Harry gets to Hogwarts, he finds things he could never have imagined. The journey from platform nine and three-quarters is a journey into mystery. It both prefigures and anticipates the final journey beyond death. The references to King's Cross in chapter 6 of the first book and chapter 35 of the last book form an *inclusio*; that is, a literary device by which a narrative is, as it were, bookended by the same reference. But it is not merely a literary device here: it is also a statement of our destiny being included in our setting off—the seed, as it might be, of what will become of us. As T. S. Eliot wrote, "The end is where we start from. . . . And the end of all our exploring / Will be to arrive where we started / And know the place for the first time."[202] JK expresses this same concept of the final meaning already implicit at the beginning, and the meaning implicit in the beginning being revealed at the end, by having Dumbledore write on the Snitch he bequeaths to Harry *I open at the close.*[203]

In eternity, which is God's point of view, everything is already there at the beginning. In time, which is our point of view, one who is at the beginning discovers what is already there, but not known to him, by traveling to the end. Through the journey of time he enters into eternity—goes to God. In fictional narrative, this implicitness of eternity in the beginning can be expressed by putting the same thing at the beginning and the end of the story, and opening up its meaning clearly at the end: by opening at the close.

A banquet or party is one symbol of heaven. Another one, which is also in the Bible, is healing. The Book of Revelation contains a vision of "the river of the water of life" and "on either side of the river is the tree of life with its twelve kinds of fruit, producing its fruit each month; and the leaves of the tree are for the healing of the nations."[204] Heaven is where God is—and where God is, there is perfect wholeness and thus complete healing. This is reflected in Dumbledore's state when he is beyond this world. He is "sprightly and upright" and his hands are "both whole and white and undamaged."[205] The Book of Revelation says of heaven: "Nothing accursed will be found there any more,"[206] so naturally even "a curse of extraordinary power,"[207] such as the one that affected Dumbledore's hand, is now powerless. It is perhaps also an indication of healing that Harry is "not wearing glasses any more."[208] In the narrative, these symbols of heaven insert the life beyond into this life.

My niece told me that she found this chapter ("King's Cross")[209] the least plausible in the series, but I replied that I found it the most plausible. As a priest, I have heard from several people about their near-death experiences. These have involved people being told that their time had not yet come, and in one instance the person returning was aware of coming back to fulfill a particular mission. There was a discussion around a table about whether to return or not. Experiences such as this one have been documented.[210] Good and bad experiences are reported. Characteristically, the good experiences are associated with peace and light: a light which is brighter than can normally be borne, but which does not hurt the eyes. This corresponds with what Harry experiences in "King's Cross." There he observes that happiness "seems to radiate from Dumbledore like light."[211]

COURAGE AND FEAR IN THE FACE OF MYSTERY

JK does not describe directly a bad experience of life beyond, but she allows it to be understood that it exists by her description of what the fragment of Voldemort's soul released becomes: "a small naked child, curled on the ground, its skin raw and rough, flayed-looking."[212] That the major portion of Voldemort's soul could have an even worse time is indicated by Dumbledore's comment to Harry that he has less to fear than Voldemort in returning to where they are.[213] These experiences belong to a realm outside normal life, whether that is the normality of the Burrow or of Privet

Drive. Harry articulates the question that the experiences raise: "Is this real? Or has this been happening inside my head?" Dumbledore replies, "Of course it is happening inside your head, Harry, but why on earth should that mean that it is not real?"[214] This reply allows a certain ambiguity to attach to what has been described. It could be that what has happened is purely subjective, but then again it could relate to a reality that is outside the normal parameters of space and time because it partakes of eternity, and for that reason is more objective than what we think of as reality. What remains true in either case is that here is a mystery, a mystery that "the brave of heart"[215] who belong to Gryffindor are not afraid to confront.

Tom Riddle is afraid to confront it. His goal is "to conquer death."[216] The whole Death Eater ethos is driven by fear of death. Voldemort's reign of terror comes from his fear of dying. Essentially, it is mystery itself that he fears. Dumbledore explains: "It is the unknown we fear when we look upon death and darkness, nothing more."[217] Harry learns this wisdom; Riddle does not. The two are explicitly compared and contrasted. They have the same sort of background, and the same educational opportunities. It is Riddle himself who points this out, as though—from the narrator's point of view—to make it clear that it is his choice that makes Riddle who he is, not his background:

> "There are strange likenesses between us, Harry Potter. Even you must have noticed. Both half-bloods, orphans, raised by Muggles. Probably the only two Parselmouths to come to Hogwarts since the great Slytherin himself. We even *look* something alike."[218]

Of course, Harry being a Parselmouth comes from the fragment of Riddle's soul in him, but this link only serves to emphasize Harry's courageous commitment to an approach different from Riddle's. Riddle's approach is born of fear, not courage. When he and Harry duel in the graveyard, and the forms of his victims that have emerged from his wand prowl around him, his face is "livid with fear."[219] Dumbledore, speaking to Harry in "King's Cross," explains the difference between the two combatants:

> "He was more afraid than you were that night, Harry. You had accepted, even embraced, the possibility of death, something Lord Voldemort has never been able to do. Your courage won."[220]

The fourth book, as mentioned earlier, is the pivotal one of the series, and this duel in the graveyard is the pivotal struggle in the series. Obviously, it is a struggle between Harry and Voldemort, but it is also a struggle between two attitudes to the possibility of death: Harry's, which accepts or even embraces it, and Voldemort's, which fears it so much he will stop at nothing in his ultimately futile attempts to avoid it. This pivotal struggle echoes and anticipates those of the first and last book respectively.

In the first book, Voldemort commits the atrocity of getting his servant to drink Unicorn blood to strengthen him. It gives him enough strength to confront Harry, threatening him with death: "Better save your own life and join me…or you'll meet the same end as your parents." Harry bravely resists the threat, answering the demand "give me the Stone" with the response "NEVER!"[221] In the final book, Harry consciously accepts "that he must die,"[222] and lives, while Voldemort, who has never accepted that he must die, dies.[223] Ultimately this struggle not only to the death but *about* death—which begins in the Chamber below the trap-door in the presence of Quirrell, is pursued in the graveyard in the presence of the Death Eaters, and is consummated in the Great Hall in the presence of the entire Hogwarts community—is a struggle between a believing and an unbelieving attitude to death. Harry fights for faith, a faith that comes from the Christian tradition.

Harry, unlike Voldemort, has that sweetness of life, recommended to Claudio by the Duke (disguised as a friar) in Shakespeare's *Measure for Measure*:

> Be absolute for death: either death or life
> Shall thereby be the sweeter.[224]

Harry's willingness to die indeed gives him a sweetness of life with Ginny and his children, which we see in the epilogue to the series, but above all it gives him a spiritual freedom. He is not "bound in to saucy doubts and fears" as a Shakespearean character not unlike Voldemort puts it.[225] Claudio moves from the attitude of Voldemort (at least in germ) to that of Harry, and his description of this transition neatly sums up the difference in the two attitudes:

> To sue to live, I find I seek to die,
> And seeking death, find life.[226]

ETERNAL DEATH

Voldemort aims to live at all costs, but in practice, this is seeking death, which comes to him; Harry in going to meet Voldemort in the forest seeks death and finds life. This contrast of attitude is clear in the dialogue Harry has with the centaur Firenze in the forbidden forest. Firenze explains:

"The blood of a unicorn will keep you alive, even if you are an inch from death, but at a terrible price. You have slain something pure and defenseless to save yourself and you will have but a half life, a cursed life, from the moment the blood touches your lips."[227]

Harry's response, with which Firenze agrees, is, "If you're going to be cursed for ever, death's better, isn't it?"[228] Voldemort exemplifies the gospel saying alluded to earlier in this book: "Those who want to save their life will lose it."[229]

Hagrid makes an interesting comment about Voldemort and death: "Dunno if he had enough human left in him to die."[230] This relates to what happened to Voldemort after his encounter with the baby Harry and his parents at Godric's Hollow, and it implies that a courageous acceptance of death is part of being fully human. The craven flight from death is a diminishment of human life, as the gospel says. Voldemort just does not see it this way. He sees his clinging to life at the expense of his "eternal jewel" (to use Macbeth's phrase for his soul)[231] as a sign of magical greatness. His idea of greatness is given by the words at the foot of the new statue at the ministry when it is under his control: "Magic is might."[232] Speaking of and to his followers, he claims such greatness:

"How could they have believed that I would not rise again? They, who knew the steps I took long ago, to guard myself against mortal death? They, who had seen proofs of the immensity of my power, in the times when I was mightier than any wizard living?"[233]

But Voldemort betrays himself in his speech. *Mortal death* draws attention to what he has not guarded against: immortal death, the "second death" spoken of by the Book of Revelation, the death that is eternal, whose image is being "thrown into the lake of fire."[234] Similarly, by describing the gathering around the cauldron in which he rises again as his "rebirthing party,"[235] he calls attention to the fact that his rebirth can never be more than an evil parody of that spoken of by the Lord of Life: "Except a man be born again, he cannot see the kingdom of God."[236] This, unlike Voldemort's, is a spiritual rebirth. "That which is born of the flesh is flesh; and that which is born of the Spirit is spirit."[237] Voldemort eschews a spiritual rebirth (he is, in fact, offered the possibility by Harry at the end).[238] He chooses, on the contrary, to be reborn of the flesh, or, as is spelled out (pun intended), to be reborn of flesh, blood, and bone.[239] Ignoring the gospel invitation to "eternal life,"[240] he boasts that he has "gone further than anybody along the path that leads to immortality." He tells his followers, "You know my goal—to conquer death."[241] In fact, like the first two brothers in the tale,[242] he is conquered by death. His quest is an evil parody of what is undertaken by the Lord of Life, the true conqueror of death, whose accomplishment is echoed by Harry's winning sacrifice.

Voldemort's sick view of death is illuminated by contrast not only with Harry's view but also with Dumbledore's. The dialogue of the two men in the ministry at the end of the fifth book is revealing. Voldemort snarls, "There is nothing worse than death." Then, "as lightly as though they were discussing the matter over drinks," Dumbledore replies, "You are quite wrong," echoing the response of Jesus to the Sadducees denying the resurrection.[243] The manner of their speaking shows which attitude is more conducive to serenity and happiness. Dumbledore is explicit in his critique of

Voldemort's attitude: "Your failure to understand that there are things much worse than death has always been your greatest weakness."[244] Voldemort thinks of his control of death as being strength; Dumbledore knows that prioritizing this control is weakness. It means that Voldemort is not a free wizard. He is forced by this priority into behaviors that damage his soul. He repeatedly tears his soul apart, by killing to create a Horcrux, "an object in which a person has concealed part of their soul."[245] In doing this he chooses a life to which, as Slughorn says, "death would be preferable."[246] And he does not escape with his life either. He may boast, "I have never died"[247] but die he does, "killed by his own rebounding curse."[248] His very attempt to remove threats to his life in the end takes it. His failure to prefer death to some things kills him.

EATING DEATH

The sick cruelty of those who are limited by a lack of trust in what is beyond life is not confined to Lord Voldemort. There is a whole culture of it. This is embodied in the Death Eaters. From the point of view of Voldemort and his followers, the phrase *Death Eater* means one who is nourished by the deaths of others. Their power and, in their own eyes, their greatness comes from the dominance that this killing gives them. But there is another interpretation of *Death Eater* that belongs to the larger narrative. These people eat death in the way that Adam and Eve ate death in the Garden of Eden. Adam and Eve ate, in John Milton's words, "the fruit / Of that forbidden tree, whose mortal taste / Brought death into the world, and all our woe, / With loss of Eden."[249] They do this because they are told by the serpent that it will enable them to "be like God, knowing good and evil."[250] In other words, they can decide for themselves what is right and wrong, without any reference to a higher authority. This, of course, is what Voldemort wants: the naked exercise of his power without reference to mercy, pity, or peace. And in this he is influenced by Slytherin: the slithery-serpent type who speaks with snakes.[251] He is the "heir of Salazar Slytherin."[252] His grandfather identifies the family as "his last living descendants."[253] He can talk to snakes. This connects him to Slytherin and both of them to Eve, who was the first to talk to a snake, and who ate the apple, and with it ate death.[254]

So the Death Eaters are connected to what in the Christian tradition is called original sin: the first sin of the race that brought about separation from the supreme good and consequent death. That sin comes from not trusting God, not trusting that his command not to eat the fruit was for our good. This same lack of trust characterizes Voldemort's failure to believe in (to use Hermione's words) "living beyond death, living after death"[255]—or, to put it in Christian terms, his failure to believe in the gospel. Among the Death Eaters, there is a culture of mistrust. The word *culture* is, of course, not used in the sense that denotes what makes a person refined or well educated. The lack of this kind of culture among Death Eaters is comically highlighted by Amycus Carrow's response to the question of the eagle-shaped door knocker that guards the entrance to the Ravenclaw common room. The door knocker's "soft, musical voice" asks, "Where do vanished objects go?" In reply, an "uncouth voice" snarls, "I dunno, do I? Shut it!"[256] Carrow and his sister Alecto "like punishment," as Neville reports.[257]

Cruelty is connected with an inability to have any grasp of what is "beyond death."[258] It is a raging against the emptiness that a lack of trust assumes is all there is beyond sight. Professor McGonagall's "nicely phrased" answer to the doorknocker's question about where what is vanished goes contains a cultured and confident counterpoint to Amycus's ignorant outburst. "Into non-being, which is to say, everything," she says.[259] This amounts to saying "into God" since God is beyond being and sustains everything in being. He alone transcends everything and is immanent in everything. Professor McGonagall is implying (at least to those who have an understanding of theology, among whom we must include the Ravenclaw door knocker) that what disappears returns to its Creator. It follows, then, that when we die we return to God. This confidence that in the "Father's house there are many dwelling places"[260] is the opposite of the desperate unbelief that drives the cruelty of the Death Eaters.

For them, "There is no good and evil, there is only power, and those too weak to seek it."[261] Their philosophy (again, not in the sense that implies education!) is redolent of that of the Nazis. There is perhaps an echo of the Nazi salute in the description of how Yaxley and Snape get through "the pair of impressive wrought-iron gates" barring their way to Malfoy Manor:

> Neither of them broke step: in silence both raised their left arms in a kind of salute and passed straight through as though the dark metal were smoke.[262]

More clearly, what Harry sees in the Pensieve in chapter 30 of the fourth book recalls the trials that followed the Second World War. Karkaroff reveals to a court the names of collaborators with the death-devoted regime, echoing the court that convened at Nuremberg.[263] Power is brought to justice. Harry's witness of this parallels the experience of those (including myself) who grew up in the aftermath of the Second World War and only gradually learned what had been involved. In the grainy black and white movies shown in the cinema, we learned something of the reign of death. For Harry, and also for us, this is not just history, however. He has to fight the power of this evil again himself. He does so with weakness. The exploration of this apparent paradox is the subject of the next chapter.

Notes

1. Deuteronomy 30:15 (RSV).
2. *The Philosopher's Stone*, 189.
3. *The Philosopher's Stone*, 216.
4. *The Goblet of Fire*, 553.
5. *The Order of the Phoenix*, 761.
6. *The Order of the Phoenix*, 398.
7. *The Deathly Hallows*, 556.
8. *The Half-Blood Prince*, 257.
9. *The Order of the Phoenix*, 712.
10. *The Order of the Phoenix*, 756.
11. *The Order of the Phoenix*, 757–59.
12. *The Deathly Hallows*, 316–17.
13. *The Goblet of Fire*, 605.
14. *The Deathly Hallows*, 72.
15. *The Deathly Hallows*, 7, quoting Aeschylus, *The Libation Bearers*.
16. *The Philosopher's Stone*, 27.
17. *The Philosopher's Stone*, 45.
18. *The Deathly Hallows*, 7, quoting Aeschylus, *The Libation Bearers*.
19. *The Goblet of Fire*, chapter 30.
20. *The Goblet of Fire*, 553.
21. *The Goblet of Fire*, 67.
22. *The Prisoner of Azkaban*, 135.

23. *The Prisoner of Azkaban*, 190.

24. *The Goblet of Fire*, 375.

25. *The Goblet of Fire*, 68.

26. *The Goblet of Fire*, 69.

27. *The Goblet of Fire*, 553.

28. *The Goblet of Fire*, 554.

29. *The Goblet of Fire*, 583.

30. *The Order of the Phoenix*, 726.

31. *The Prisoner of Azkaban*, 277.

32. *The Prisoner of Azkaban*, 278.

33. *The Prisoner of Azkaban*, 277.

34. *The Deathly Hallows*, 7, quoting Aeschylus, *The Libation Bearers*.

35. *The Philosopher's Stone*, 15.

36. *The Philosopher's Stone*, 92.

37. *The Order of the Phoenix*, 547.

38. *The Philosopher's Stone*, 48.

39. *The Half-Blood Prince*, 568.

40. *The Deathly Hallows*, 461.

41. *The Half-Blood Prince*, 568.

42. These are explored in my book *Paradise on Earth: Exploring a Christian Response to Suffering* (Stowmarket, UK: Kevin Mayhew Publishers, 1993).

43. *The Deathly Hallows*, 7, quoting Aeschylus, *The Libation Bearers*.

44. *The Prisoner of Azkaban*, 10.

45. *The Deathly Hallows*, 52.

46. *The Deathly Hallows*, 69.

47. *The Deathly Hallows*, 70.

48. *The Deathly Hallows*, 385.

49. *The Goblet of Fire*, 131.

50. *The Goblet of Fire*, 136–37.

51. *The Deathly Hallows*, 115–16.

52. *The Deathly Hallows*, 487.

53. *The Deathly Hallows*, 511–12.
54. *The Philosopher's Stone*, 70.
55. *The Chamber of Secrets*, 75 and 87.
56. *The Deathly Hallows*, 556.
57. *The Deathly Hallows*, 176.
58. *The Half-Blood Prince*, 149.
59. *The Deathly Hallows*, 596.
60. *The Deathly Hallows*, 528.
61. *The Deathly Hallows*, 545.
62. *The Deathly Hallows*, 528.
63. *The Deathly Hallows*, 549.
64. *The Order of the Phoenix*, 759.
65. *The Order of the Phoenix*, 157–59.
66. *The Order of the Phoenix*, 160.
67. *The Prisoner of Azkaban*, 197.
68. *The Deathly Hallows*, 499.
69. *The Deathly Hallows*, 485.
70. *The Deathly Hallows*, 469.
71. *The Goblet of Fire*, 168.
72. *The Deathly Hallows*, 487, and *The Order of the Phoenix*, 161.
73. *The Deathly Hallows*, 332.
74. *The Philosopher's Stone*, 77.
75. *The Philosopher's Stone*, 161.
76. *The Philosopher's Stone*, 215.
77. *The Deathly Hallows*, 599.
78. *The Half-Blood Prince*, chapter 3.
79. *The Half-Blood Prince*, 158.
80. *The Half-Blood Prince*, 529.
81. *The Half-Blood Prince*, 58.
82. *The Deathly Hallows*, 546.
83. *The Half-Blood Prince*, 547–48.
84. *The Philosopher's Stone*, 197.
85. *The Order of the Phoenix*, 720.

86. *The Deathly Hallows*, 577.

87. *The Deathly Hallows*, 564.

88. *The Deathly Hallows*, 577.

89. *The Deathly Hallows*, 554.

90. Revelation 2:11.

91. *The Deathly Hallows*, 578.

92. *The Deathly Hallows*, 346.

93. *The Deathly Hallows*, 333.

94. *The Deathly Hallows*, 348.

95. *The Deathly Hallows*, 392.

96. Luke 9:24.

97. *The Deathly Hallows*, 596.

98. Luke 11:9.

99. *The Philosopher's Stone*, 217.

100. *The Deathly Hallows*, 559.

101. *The Deathly Hallows*, 560.

102. *The Deathly Hallows*, 331.

103. *The Deathly Hallows*, 332.

104. *The Deathly Hallows*, 561–64.

105. *The Deathly Hallows*, 269, and 1 Corinthians 15:26 (King James Version).

106. *The Deathly Hallows*, 332.

107. *The Deathly Hallows*, 571.

108. *The Deathly Hallows*, 569.

109. *The Deathly Hallows*, 7.

110. 1 Corinthians 13:12.

111. 1 Corinthians 15:20.

112. John 1:5.

113. Matthew 28:1–6.

114. *The Deathly Hallows*, 595.

115. John 1:5.

116. *The Deathly Hallows*, 595.

117. *The Deathly Hallows*, 596.

118. *The Chamber of Secrets*, 215.

119. *Hamlet*, act 1, scene I, lines 158–64.
120. *The Chamber of Secrets*, 216.
121. *The Chamber of Secrets*, 217.
122. *The Chamber of Secrets*, 219.
123. *The Chamber of Secrets*, 155.
124. Isaiah 53:2.
125. *The Chamber of Secrets*, 155.
126. Isaiah 53:4.
127. *The Chamber of Secrets*, 155.
128. Isaiah 53:5.
129. *The Chamber of Secrets*, 155.
130. *The Chamber of Secrets*, 234.
131. Genesis 3:1.
132. John Milton, *Paradise Lost*, Book 1, line 3.
133. *The Chamber of Secrets*, 235.
134. *The Deathly Hallows*, 594.
135. *The Chamber of Secrets*, 236.
136. *The Deathly Hallows*, 596.
137. *The Deathly Hallows*, 276.
138. *The Deathly Hallows*, 20.
139. *The Philosopher's Stone*, 63.
140. *The Half-Blood Prince*, 70.
141. *The Deathly Hallows*, 560.
142. *The Deathly Hallows*, 607.
143. *The Order of the Phoenix*, 565.
144. *The Deathly Hallows*, 307, and *The Half-Blood Prince*, 78.
145. *The Half-Blood Prince*, 532.
146. *The Deathly Hallows*, 307.
147. *The Half-Blood Prince*, 40.
148. *The Deathly Hallows*, 581.
149. *The Deathly Hallows*, 77.
150. *The Order of the Phoenix*, 667.
151. *The Goblet of Fire*, 448.

152. *The Philosopher's Stone*, 102.
153. *The Half-Blood Prince*, 40.
154. *The Deathly Hallows*, 528.
155. *The Deathly Hallows*, chapter 33.
156. *The Deathly Hallows*, 393 and 411.
157. *The Order of the Phoenix*, 140.
158. *The Goblet of Fire*, 553.
159. *The Deathly Hallows*, 7.
160. *The Chamber of Secrets*, 236–37.
161. Genesis 3:1–24.
162. *The Chamber of Secrets*, 239.
163. *The Chamber of Secrets*, 232.
164. *The Goblet of Fire*, 575.
165. *The Goblet of Fire*, 576.
166. *The Goblet of Fire*, 576.
167. *The Goblet of Fire*, 577.
168. *The Goblet of Fire*, 605.
169. Shakespeare, *Hamlet*, act 1, scene 5, line 166.
170. *The Goblet of Fire*, 577–79.
171. *The Goblet of Fire*, 605.
172. *The Goblet of Fire*, 606.
173. *The Goblet of Fire*, 548.
174. *The Order of the Phoenix*, 549.
175. *The Order of the Phoenix*, 719.
176. *The Order of the Phoenix*, 740.
177. Shakespeare, *Merchant of Venice*, act 5, scene 1, line 64.
178. *The Half-Blood Prince*, 573.
179. *The Deathly Hallows*, 7.
180. *The Half-Blood Prince*, 589.
181. *The Order of the Phoenix*, 65.
182. *The Order of the Phoenix*, 718.
183. *The Order of the Phoenix*, 760–61.
184. *The Order of the Phoenix*, 682–83.
185. *The Order of the Phoenix*, 710–11.

186. *The Order of the Phoenix*, 747.

187. *The Order of the Phoenix*, 759.

188. *The Deathly Hallows*, 266.

189. Matthew 6:21 (King James Version).

190. Matthew 6:20 (King James Version).

191. *The Deathly Hallows*, 268, and 1 Corinthians 15:26 (King James Version).

192. 1 Corinthians 15:22 (King James Version).

193. 1 Corinthians 15:24 (King James Version).

194. *The Deathly Hallows*, 90.

195. *The Deathly Hallows*, chapter 35.

196. *The Deathly Hallows*, 570.

197. Isaiah 25:6–8.

198. *The Deathly Hallows*, 268, and 1 Corinthians 15:26.

199. *The Philosopher's Stone*, chapter 6.

200. *The Deathly Hallows*, 578.

201. *The Philosopher's Stone*, 69.

202. T. S. Eliot, *Little Gidding*, Part V, in *Collected Poems, 1909–1962* (London: Faber and Faber), 221, 222.

203. *The Deathly Hallows*, 113.

204. Revelation 22:1–2.

205. *The Deathly Hallows*, 566.

206. Revelation 22:3.

207. *The Deathly Hallows*, 546.

208. *The Deathly Hallows*, 565.

209. *The Deathly Hallows*, chapter 35.

210. See, for example, Margot Grey, *Return From Death: An Exploration of the Near-Death Experience* (London: Arkana, 1985).

211. *The Deathly Hallows*, 567.

212. *The Deathly Hallows*, 566.

213. *The Deathly Hallows*, 578.

214. *The Deathly Hallows*, 579.

215. *The Philosopher's Stone*, 88.

216. *The Goblet of Fire*, 566.

217. *The Half-Blood Prince*, 529.

218. *The Chamber of Secrets*, 233.

219. *The Goblet of Fire*, 579.

220. *The Deathly Hallows*, 569.

221. *The Philosopher's Stone*, 213.

222. *The Deathly Hallows*, 556.

223. *The Deathly Hallows*, 596.

224. Shakespeare, *Measure for Measure*, act 3, scene 1, lines 5–6.

225. Shakespeare, *Macbeth*, act 3, scene 4, lines 23–24.

226. Shakespeare, *Measure for Measure*, act 3, scene 1, lines 42–43.

227. *The Philosopher's Stone*, 188.

228. *The Philosopher's Stone*, 189.

229. Luke 9:24.

230. *The Philosopher's Stone*, 46.

231. Shakespeare, *Macbeth*, act 3, scene 1, line 67.

232. *The Deathly Hallows*, 198.

233. *The Goblet of Fire*, 562.

234. Revelation 20:14–15.

235. *The Goblet of Fire*, 565.

236. John 3:3 (King James Version).

237. John 3:6 (King James Version).

238. *The Deathly Hallows*, 594.

239. *The Goblet of Fire*, 556–57.

240. John 3:15.

241. *The Goblet of Fire*, 566.

242. *The Deathly Hallows*, 331–32.

243. Matthew 22:29.

244. *The Order of the Phoenix*, 718.

245. *The Half-Blood Prince*, 464.

246. *The Half-Blood Prince*, 465.

247. *The Goblet of Fire*, 575.

248. *The Deathly Hallows*, 596.
249. John Milton, *Paradise Lost*, Book 1, lines 1–4.
250. Genesis 3:5.
251. *The Chamber of Secrets*, 147.
252. *The Chamber of Secrets*, 233.
253. *The Half-Blood Prince*, 196.
254. Genesis, chapter 3.
255. *The Deathly Hallows*, 269.
256. *The Deathly Hallows*, 475.
257. *The Deathly Hallows*, 461.
258. *The Deathly Hallows*, 269.
259. *The Deathly Hallows*, 476.
260. John 14:2.
261. *The Philosopher's Stone*, 211.
262. *The Deathly Hallows*, 9.
263. *The Goblet of Fire*, 511–13.

5

Power Is Made Perfect in Weakness

POWER AND WEAKNESS

The very first chapter of the series—"The Boy Who Lived"[1]—is about how weakness defeats power. JK, mistress of prolepsis, is telling us in the very beginning about the final denouement at the end of the series. In this, Harry, weak and defenseless, walks into the Death Eaters' camp in the forest and allows Voldemort to use a Killing Curse on him.[2] He is, once more, the boy who lived. The final time that Voldemort uses the Killing Curse on him, in the Great Hall, Harry is, a third time, the boy who lived. He himself does not use a Killing Curse: Voldemort is "killed by his own rebounding curse."[3] This time Voldemort's defeat is final. The celebration of Voldemort's first defeat (by the baby Harry) is chronicled in the beginning of the first book, which tells of indiscreet gatherings in front of Muggles;[4] this is echoed in the penultimate chapter of the last book, which tells of "the screams and the cheers and the roars" of those who have seen Voldemort's final defeat.[5]

However, the difference between the first defeat of Voldemort's power and his final defeat is not just the difference between a battle won and a war won, it is a difference between defeat by an involuntary and unconscious weakness and defeat by a voluntary and conscious weakness. All proper reservations made, we might say it is the difference between Christmas and Easter. The whole of the series is about Harry growing from this involuntary and unconscious weakness to a voluntary and conscious weakness. It shows how, ultimately, power is defeated by weakness. To understand this, we need to look more closely at the first chapter of the series and its presentation of weakness defeating power, of the boy who lived.

Baby Harry, the Manger, and the Cross

Earlier, in chapter 3 of this book, I cited the series' first statement about the defeat of Voldemort by the baby Harry, made by Professor McGonagall. This is a statement worth repeating:

> "They're saying he tried to kill the Potters' son, Harry. But—he couldn't. He couldn't kill that little boy. No one knows why, or how, but they're saying that when he couldn't kill Harry Potter, Voldemort's power somehow broke—and that's why he's gone."[6]

At this point no one knows what caused Voldemort's power to break: even Dumbledore says, "We can only guess.... We may never know."[7] It is not until Harry witnesses Voldemort talking to his Death Eaters in the graveyard, in the pivotal scene of the series, that we hear Voldemort himself explain it: "I miscalculated, my friends, I admit it. My curse was deflected by the woman's foolish sacrifice, and it rebounded upon me."[8] Unlike Harry, Voldemort does not learn, and his magic becomes vulnerable to the sacrifice of that woman's son, who is able to tell him at the end, "I've done what my mother did."[9] The theme of sacrifice will be explored fully in the next chapter.

Here it is relevant to the identification of the defining archetype of weakness defeating power: the sacrifice of Christ on the cross, defeating the power of the devil. This identification gives greater resonance to Professor McGonagall's statement about Voldemort, quoted above: "He couldn't kill that little boy." This evokes the failure of King Herod to kill the baby Jesus. Jesus escapes because his foster father Joseph is alerted by an angel.[10] When Professor McGonagall asks, "How in the name of heaven did [the baby] survive?"[11] the use of the word *heaven* echoes this intervention from heaven in the archetypal story. It is itself echoed in the final magical confrontation between Harry and Voldemort, when Harry yells "his best hope to the heavens."[12]

The first unconscious confrontation that Harry has with Voldemort is linked to the final fully aware confrontation with him, not only by Voldemort's explanation in the graveyard at the turning point of the series, but also by the identification of them both with the sacrifice of Christ. Already as a little boy, Harry's destiny is to offer himself as a victim. This echoes traditional Christian iconography, which often shows the baby Jesus with a foreshadowing of the passion—such as three nails in the background. The gospels' depiction of Jesus as a little baby proclaims that "God's weakness is stronger than human strength,"[13] as Saint Paul puts it, but also in the last book of the Bible, Jesus is presented as triumphant over evil in his weakness.

The visionary John is told, "See, the Lion of the tribe of Judah, the Root of David, has conquered." John looks and reports seeing a different animal. He sees "a Lamb standing as if it had been slaughtered."[14] The Lion is the symbol of triumph, but when the seer looks more closely at how this triumph is effected, he sees a symbol of weakness, of helpless and oppressed innocence—a slaughtered Lamb. However, the Lamb is standing: "God's weakness is stronger than human strength,"[15] and he has conquered death through the cross.

JK describes the same victory: first proleptically in baby Harry's survival of Voldemort's attack on his family home, and then definitively in his final battle with the One Who Wants Death, and who spreads death. She is doing the same thing that C. S. Lewis does when he shows us the lion Aslan being sacrificed on a stone table to defeat the evil power of the witch in *The Lion, the Witch, and the Wardrobe*. However, despite the fact that JK's language and the books' general context of witchcraft and wizardry are apparently less Christian than that of Lewis (who reserves witchcraft for evil), her depiction of this victory of weakness over power is actually more faithful to the fullness of the Christian tradition than Lewis's. Aslan, it is true, suffers the weakness of being bound and killed, but he is always a lion. There is a relative absence of that aspect of God's victory that Christian tradition has seen as being expressed by this verse from the prophet Isaiah:

> He was oppressed, and he was afflicted,
>   yet he did not open his mouth;
> like a lamb that is led to the slaughter,
>   and like a sheep that before its shearers is silent,
>   so he did not open his mouth.[16]

THE SCAR AND THE PRECIOUS WOUNDS

This aspect of the victory makes sense of the question that puzzles Harry when he first learns that he is a wizard and that he has diminished Voldemort's power. He has spent his life "being clouted by Dudley and bullied by Aunt Petunia and Uncle Vernon." If he really is a wizard, he thinks,

> why hadn't they been turned into warty toads every time they'd tried to lock him in his cupboard? If he'd once defeated the greatest sorcerer in the world, how come Dudley had always been able to kick him around like a football?[17]

The answer is in the Christian tradition: Harry triumphs through his suffering, just as Dumbledore sacrifices blood to enter the cave where Voldemort has hidden the locket Horcrux.[18] The answer is in the scar that Harry received. Hagrid tells him:

> "That was no ordinary cut. That's what yeh get when a powerful, evil curse touches yeh—took care of yer mum an' dad an' yer house, even—but it didn't work on you, an that's why yer famous, Harry."[19]

The magical world is set free by this wounding of Harry. It corresponds to the words that the Christian tradition has applied to the wounding of Christ:

> He was wounded for our transgressions,
>   crushed for our iniquities;
> upon him was the punishment that made us whole.[20]

The fascination Fred and George show at Harry's scar[21] corresponds to the need of that other twin, Thomas, to see "the mark of the nails."[22] Christmas, as was mentioned above, is to the forefront in the series, but the scar points to Good Friday and its suffering. Already, it gives something of the protection that the ultimate sacrifice gives. Because Voldemort's power has been broken, he is unable to return without help. However, there remains the possibility of choosing to cooperate with evil, as the man with two faces does in the first book of the series.[23] This reflects the reality that the Christian faith presents us with: it is possible to choose evil even though a victory has been won over evil for those who elect to claim it in the name of the Savior.

CONDITIONAL AND ULTIMATE TRIUMPH OF GOOD

There are two levels on which the Harry Potter books can be read: from within the story (corresponding to a first reading) or as a whole (corresponding to subsequent readings). On the first level, the victory of baby Harry (as a baby) over Voldemort is conditional on the wizards' refusal to cooperate with him; this corresponds to the Christian understanding that, while we are still living in time, we remain liable to be tempted to cooperate with the devil. On the second level, the victory of Harry (as a man) over Voldemort is final; this corresponds to the Christian understanding that, in the fullness of time, God wins an eternal victory over the devil. The view of the reader who has read the whole of the series and is rereading it is like that of the believer who knows by faith that, as Julian of Norwich said, "All will be well." He or she has, of course, read the last words: "All was well."[24]

This does not alter the fact that living in time, and struggling to conquer in our weakness, is not an experience of satisfaction. Voldemort has that sort of experience, but it is an illusion. After Ron has gotten the Sword of Gryffindor out of the icy lake, destroyed the locket Horcrux, and saved Harry's life, his dialogue with Harry tells it like it is. In response to Harry's acknowledgement of what he has done, Ron mumbles, "That makes me sound a lot cooler than I was." Harry responds, "Stuff like that always sounds cooler than it really was."[25] Real heroism is very different from the arrogant self-sufficiency of Voldemort. It is an experience of one's weakness, even wretchedness. It is precisely here that the good triumphs, that God triumphs, because the human ego is sidelined and, in the space thereby created, good can be sovereign, God can act. Saint Paul makes this point when he reports being told by the Lord of Life, "Power is made perfect in weakness."[26] He draws from this the conclusion: "Whenever I am weak, then I am strong."[27]

WEAKNESS ENABLING THE STRENGTH OF LOVE

One of the ways in which this apparent paradox is shown to be true in ordinary life is in the way people relate to each other. A certain weakness, a certain vulnerability toward the other, engenders a relationship of trust in which help and support are gained: this help might well be refused to one who tried to bully the other into giving it. JK dramatizes this truth about human life by showing Dumbledore, Harry, and others triumphing over Voldemort's untrusting hardness with their trusting weakness. This dynamic can work even with people who seem to be total enemies. In the third book, Harry spares Pettigrew's life, because he thinks his father would want him to do that.[28] Pettigrew later escapes.[29] Harry is cast down about this, but Dumbledore takes a positive view of his clemency. He says to Harry, "You did a very noble thing, in saving Pettigrew's life."[30] He explains how this apparent weakness creates a bond that actually empowers Harry in his struggle with Voldemort:

> "Pettigrew owes his life to you. You have sent Voldemort a deputy who is in your debt. When one wizard saves another wizard's life, it creates a certain bond between them…and I'm much mistaken if Voldemort wants his servant in the debt of Harry Potter."

Harry doesn't want a bond with Pettigrew, but Dumbledore insists:

> "This is magic at its deepest, its most impenetrable, Harry. But trust me….The time may come when you will be very glad you saved Pettigrew's life."[31]

The deep and impenetrable magic is that of mercy and forgiveness: it is that of Jesus on the cross saying, "Father, forgive them; for they do not know what they are doing."[32] It is, ultimately, the magic of love, "a force that is at once more wonderful and more terrible than death, than human intelligence, than the forces of nature."[33] The force that bonds one person with another is, ultimately, stronger than the force that terrorizes or bullies another person into obedience. Politically, it is sometimes called "soft power" to distinguish it from military power. On the personal level, according to the Bible, it is "strong as death," for "many waters cannot quench love, neither can floods drown it."[34]

The next chapter will examine JK's presentation of love more fully: here its discussion is apposite to show how her narrative demonstrates that, indeed, "power is made perfect in weakness."[35]

Nearly four years after Harry has saved Pettigrew's life, he finds himself being throttled by the silver hand with which Voldemort replaced the hand that Pettigrew sacrificed to give the Dark Lord a body. Harry protests: "You're going to kill me?…After I saved your life? You owe me, Wormtail!"[36] Then the magic happens: the silver fingers slacken. This "tiny, merciful impulse" is enough to save Harry's life. The magical hand responds by doing the work of the one who made it and throttles the one to whom it was given.[37] Harry's mercy to Pettigrew—his weakness, Voldemort would say—saves his own life and, actually, destroys his opponent. Evil tries to destroy good, but good lets evil destroy itself. Power tries to impose itself on weakness, but weakness lets power destroy itself.

Expelliarmus

This dynamic of weakness letting power destroy itself is even more evident in Harry's relationship with Voldemort. Harry appears to be much weaker than Riddle. When he first starts teaching his fellow students in Dumbledore's Army to prepare them to take on the Dark Lord and his Death Eaters, he says: "I was thinking, the first thing we should do is *Expelliarmus*, you know, the Disarming Charm. I know it's pretty basic, but I've found it really useful—" A skeptical Zacharias Smith spots the relative weakness of the charm against their enemy: "I don't think *Expelliarmus* is exactly going to help us against You-Know-Who, do you?"

However, Harry is able to reply that he has already used it against him, and that it has already saved his life.[38]

Harry is referring to the scene in the graveyard that is pivotal for the whole series. Here Harry shouts, "*Expelliarmus!*" as Voldemort cries, "*Avada Kedavra.*" A jet of red light from Harry's wand meets a jet of green light from Voldemort's wand—the colors mirroring the colors of the other's eyes—and the two jets become a single bright, deep gold. Dumbledore later explains that this happens because the wands share a core ("a feather from the tail of the same phoenix"). Each is meeting (in Sirius' phrase) "its brother," and so the wands "will not work properly against each other." In terms of magical theory, this is known as *Priori Incantatem*, or "the reverse spell effect," but in the light of the above reflections about the magical bond formed when Harry, in apparent weakness, saves Pettigrew's life, we can perhaps see a deeper magic at work.[39] By using a Disarming Charm rather than a Killing Curse, Harry is forming a bond with his adversary rather than simply trying to crush him. Indeed, we often say of someone admitting a weakness that it is "disarming."

Harry has, as it were, established a relationship with his opponent *despite* his opponent. This relationship leads to disclosure. The murders of Voldemort are revealed as the forms of his victims issue from his wand.[40] This reflects the common experience that, when we make ourselves vulnerable by being open about ourselves, others are likely to respond by being open about themselves. What happens here, however, is more than that because Harry's weakness compels, so to speak, the revelation from Voldemort. It is as though there is a divine power about this weakness, or at least a divine guarantee that it will be honored. The whole process mirrors what happens with Pettigrew and the silver hand that hesitates to take the life of the one who has spared him. It is perhaps significant that when Pettigrew dives for Lupin's dropped wand, after the latter has transformed into a werewolf, Harry's response is to yell, "*Expelliarmus!*" pointing his own wand at Pettigrew.[41] This doesn't stop Pettigrew transforming into a rat, but, as we have seen, the ultimate result of this apparently weak spell is the saving of Harry's life.

In his relations with both Pettigrew and Voldemort, Harry's weakness is triumphant. It is the triumph of the golden light that connects—the triumph of relationship, of love, of God. According to the Christian tradition, God himself, who is love,[42] establishes his reign by the weakness that invites relationship: the weakness of a baby, the weakness of a man who asks for a drink,[43] the weakness of one condemned to death, the weakness of the Lamb. This weakness invites, establishes, and nurtures relationship: love freely received and given. It is *this* that is triumphant, not force. That is so even if it meets with adamantine opposition. The inviting weakness is God's mercy; its triumph is his justice. Ultimately they are one, for God is one. God draws all into relationship, into love. The only alternative to this is self-destructive diminishment. This traditional Christian understanding informs and illumines the Harry Potter books. Without their author necessarily working out a theological underpinning for the narrative, the books are written in the context of a Christian culture, with an instinct for what is spiritually important. They show the working of Christian values in the hard cases of confrontation with evil: the evil of softness and yielding (Quirrell and Pettigrew) and the evil of hardness and blindness (Voldemort).

The ultimate confrontation is a reprise of the clash of the two spells that did battle in the graveyard, and shows once more that "love is strong as death."[44] However, before Harry comes to this final showdown in the Great Hall of Hogwarts, his repeated use of the apparently weak

Expelliarmus spell is challenged. He uses it during an aerial fight with the Death Eaters when he sees "the strangely blank face" of Stan Shunpike, the Knight Bus conductor. The spell produces an immediate response from the Death Eaters, who until this point have been confused by the six other people made to look like Harry by polyjuice potion. There is a shout from a hooded Death Eater: "That's him, it's him, it's the real one!"[45] Soon after, Voldemort himself is in pursuit.[46] When Harry is debriefed about what happened afterward, he explains that he tried to Disarm the Knight Bus conductor because "he doesn't know what he's doing, does he? He must be Imperiused!" An aghast Lupin responds, "Harry, the time for Disarming is past! These people are trying to capture and kill you! At least Stun if you aren't prepared to kill!" This reminds Harry of Zacharias Smith's response to his suggestion to Dumbledore's army that they work on *Expelliarmus*, and he tells Lupin his reasons for what he did:

> "We were hundreds of feet up! Stan's not himself, and if I stunned him and he'd fallen he'd have died the same as if I'd used *Avada Kedavra*! *Expelliarmus* saved me from Voldemort two years ago."

Lupin, however, feels that Harry is too well known for performing the spell for it to be prudent to use, and tells him: "Repeating it tonight in front of Death Eaters who either witnessed or heard about the first occasion was close to suicidal!" While not wanting Harry to kill, his advice is, "*Expelliarmus* is a useful spell, Harry, but the Death Eaters seem to think it is your signature move, and I urge you not to let it become so!" Harry's reply makes clear the difference between his approach and Voldemort's: "I won't blast people out of the way just because they're there.... That's

Voldemort's job."[47] Harry accepts the weakness of treating other people with fairness and consideration for their safety. He owns the signature spell that he was already getting very good at by the end of his second year at Hogwarts,[48] the spell he used in the maze to make the spider drop him.[49] Being seen as weak is not a problem for him.

TEARS

Voldemort, by contrast, is unwilling to accept any weakness. Even as a baby, he hardly ever cries.[50] He dislikes tears in others, a sign of their weakness or perhaps a reminder of his own. As he relives his attack on the Potters, the tears of the baby Harry remind him that "he had never been able to stomach the small ones' whining in the orphanage."[51] This extreme antipathy to tears marks him out as not belonging to human community, as not being in relationship to it. Tears indicate a heart that can soften. Draco Malfoy cries about the task Voldemort has given him.[52] He is unable to murder Dumbledore.[53] He is "not a killer," as the latter observes.[54] Harry's eyes moisten when Dumbledore speaks of his mother's love for him.[55] Ron's are wet when he has just destroyed the locket Horcrux.[56] Hermione cries when Ron says, "No one can stand her."[57] Hagrid cries in remorse over his indiscretion.[58] These are only examples.

In the Harry Potter series, tears are a sign of being human, of belonging to human community. This does not mean that they are an unlimited good, however! When the tearful Cho goes out with someone else, Ron observes to Harry: "You're well out of it, mate....I mean, she's quite good-looking and all that, but you want someone a bit more cheerful."[59] On the other hand, Ginny cries like the others at Dumbledore's funeral,[60] but not when Harry tells her they have to separate so that he can pursue Voldemort.[61] When she is about to give Harry a seventeenth-birthday kiss to remember her by, he reflects that "one of the many wonderful things about Ginny" is that she is "rarely weepy."[62] Tears are an acceptance of weakness and limitation, a refusal of the inhuman self-sufficiency that characterizes Voldemort, but they are not something you can't have too much of. Rather, as with Hermione's lonely or Hagrid's remorseful tears, they simply indicate an accepted need of others and of God. They are a sign of the weakness that, by Saint Paul's reckoning, makes us strong—the weakness that enables relationship. This weakness, as the brave and heroic deeds of the Gryffindors (such as Neville killing Nagini)[63] show, does not exclude strong action.

POWER AS AVOIDANCE OF RELATIONSHIP

Voldemort's strong action is something completely different from the strong action of heroism. His is the wielding of power to avoid relationship, power without the weakness that reaches out to others. This simply crushes others. It aims at domination. Voldemort wants "to bring the wizards out of hiding to rule the Muggles and the Muggle-borns."[64] This ambition is represented in the hideous statue of black stone that is in the Atrium of Voldemort's Ministry of Magic. It shows a witch and wizard sitting on "hundreds and hundreds of naked bodies, men, women and children, all with rather stupid, ugly faces, twisted and pressed together to support the weight of the handsomely robed wizards." It carries, "in foot-high letters," the legend "MAGIC IS MIGHT."[65] The word *magic* here is being used in a sense diametrically opposed to the sense of the word *magical* in JK's dedication of the fifth book to members of her family who, she says, make her world "magical." The magic she refers to, I think we can assume, is the magic of relationship.

Voldemort's magic is the opposite. It excludes all relationship of kinship, all kindness. "Of house-elves and children's tales, of love, loyalty and innocence, Voldemort knows and understands nothing."[66] His statue replaces "the Fountain of Magical Brethren,"[67] which symbolizes fraternal harmony and acceptance of diversity. The latter shows "a noble-looking wizard with his wand pointing straight up in the air"—not threatening anyone, but, as it were, aspiring to the highest values—and around him "a beautiful witch, a centaur, a goblin, and a house-elf."[68] That the values of fraternity and cooperation symbolized by the fountain include care for the weak is indicated by the fact that coins thrown into its pool are given "to St Mungo's Hospital for Magical Maladies and Injuries."[69] Such charity is excluded from Voldemort's world, where "there is only power and those too weak to seek it."[70]

These words are spoken by Quirrell, Voldemort's servant and pupil. Their context, however, indicates their lack of wisdom. Quirrell introduces the words by speaking about when he first met Voldemort: "A foolish young man I was then, full of ridiculous ideas about good and evil. Lord Voldemort showed me how wrong I was."[71] Quirrell's real folly is not believing in good and evil: it is trusting Voldemort. This is abundantly clear in what Voldemort later says about him. He calls him "young, foolish, and gullible" and says, "He was easy to bend to my will."[72] Quirrell is left to die by Voldemort, who "shows just as little mercy to his followers as his enemies."[73] This anticipates Voldemort killing Snape, whom he believes to be one of his followers.[74] The magic of might is everything for Voldemort—he kills Snape for mastery of the Elder Wand—but the magic of relationship, or fraternity, is nothing for him. His followers echo his attitude, as when magic is used to mock and manipulate Muggles at the Quidditch World Cup site. This attitude, is, as Ron says, "sick."[75] It is ignorant and stupid.

As one of Voldemort's victims tells him just before dying, there is so much he does not understand.[76] His attitude loses Voldemort the help of others: obviously, directly when he kills them, but also indirectly when, by refusing to trust others with his weakness, he loses the possibility of their help. It weakens him by contrast with his opponents, who work in relationship and trust and so benefit from the skill of others. Harry and Hermione, for example, trust Ron's chess-playing ability and hand control over to him, so enabling Voldemort's attempt to gain the Philosopher's Stone to be thwarted by the overcoming of the spell that barred their way to it.[77] Voldemort's failure even to imagine that others have a skill that he does not weakens him. He does not realize, for example, that Kreacher can disapparate from the cave where he has hidden his locket Horcrux. Hermione points out that he "would have considered the ways of house-elves [to be] far beneath his notice," and that he pays for the way he treats house-elves.[78]

Dumbledore pinpoints Voldemort's greatest failure in understanding what others are capable of, and he is not, when he says, "If there is one thing Voldemort cannot understand, it is love."[79] Love's power, and its efficacy against Voldemort, will be explored in the next chapter, but it is relevant to our consideration of power and weakness to note that the power of love is not available to Voldemort precisely because he cannot tolerate weakness. The vulnerability that engenders relationship, the weakness that acknowledges the need of another—whether it be chess-playing skills, or his or her magic, or simply a return of love—is absolutely intolerable to him.

For Voldemort, there are only two desired options in his dealing with another. They are indicated by what he says of Bertha Jorkins: "I could not possess her. I disposed of her."[80] Possession or disposal are the only ways he really wants to relate to others. Once he steps out of the cauldron with his own body,[81] he no longer needs to take direct possession of another's body as he did with Quirrell.[82] However, his mode of relating to people is still by treating them as his property, to be used at his will. To do this he needs power and spells. He seeks power by seeking the Elder Wand. Aptly, for such an unhallowed person, this is the only one of the Hallows that he knows about. He sees only the Hallow that cannot be hidden.[83] He knows nothing of the spiritual value (to be explored in a later chapter) of the hiddenness that is associated with the Invisibility Cloak. And he feels no longing for the communion with those who have gone before him that is associated with the Resurrection Stone. He longs only for power. Even as "a ruin of his former self," he is "still determined to regain power."[84] His lust for power is ignorance. To pursue it, the spells he uses are the Unforgivable Curses.[85] Almost as soon as he has his own body, he uses the Cruciatus Curse on Harry[86] to demonstrate (as he supposes) that he is stronger than him.[87] He Imperiuses people such as Pius Thicknesse, who runs the Ministry of Magic for him.[88] His biggest means of control, however, is also his means of disposing of people.

Avada Kedavra

Voldemort's signature spell is the Killing Curse, *Avada Kedavra*.[89] The words of this spell suggest "Have a cadaver!"—a contemptuous killing that changes hope into a corpse. But, of course, it is his own hope that Voldemort is killing. As explained above, Voldemort deals death to his own soul, inflicting on himself what the Bible calls "the second death."[90] Although Harry is criticized for his repeated use of his signature spell,[91] it is Voldemort who is truly foolish for his repeated use of his. His soul is torn to pieces as he makes Horcrux after Horcrux, and his repeated use of *Avada Kedavra*, against Harry in particular, is a repeated failure that leads him, unable to learn from his mistake, to his "mortal death," contrary to his plans and intentions.[92] His first failure—when he uses the powerful curse against Harry as a weak baby—leads to his power breaking.[93] His second failure—after he has tortured Harry twice[94]—leads to the *Priori Incantatem* (reverse spell) effect.[95] The golden beam of light that connects his wand with Harry's[96] is, as it were, the light of God convicting him of his sins: "the shadowy figures of Voldemort's victims" close in upon him like furies claiming a just revenge.[97] This is, as already mentioned, the pivotal scene of the series, and it anticipates the final use of the Killing Curse against Harry, where not just the dead, but death itself pursues and, in a final justice, finds Voldemort.[98]

Before that, however, Voldemort fails two more times in his use of the Killing Curse against Harry. He uses it against him in the Atrium of the Ministry of Magic. Dumbledore rescues Harry, and the manner of his rescue is highly significant for understanding why Voldemort in the end loses. We are told:

> The headless golden statue of the wizard in the fountain had sprung alive, leaping from its plinth to land with a crash on the floor between Harry and Voldemort. The spell merely glanced off its chest as the statue flung out its arms to protect Harry.[99]

The statue has already been under attack by Voldemort's lieutenant, Bellatrix, who has blasted off its wizard's head.[100] Both this attack and the statue's magical defense of Harry are apt. The statue, part of the Fountain of Magical Brethren,[101] represents the greatest threat to Voldemort: fraternity. The Sorting Hat has extolled the value of this in its song at the beginning of the year:

> *"Our Hogwarts is in danger*
> *From external, deadly foes*
> *And we must unite inside her*
> *Or we'll crumble from within."*[102]

This is a similar point to the one Dumbledore has made at the end of the previous year: "We are only as strong as we are united, as weak as we are divided."[103] The statue that stands between Voldemort and Harry is a symbol of unity: symbolically, unity protects Harry. This unity involves an acceptance of diversity, symbolized by the wizard, witch, centaur, goblin, and a house-elf standing together.[104] Voldemort is against diversity: "There will be no more Sorting at Hogwarts School," he says, consigning all to his own house.[105] This unity also involves a "strong bond of friendship and trust."[106] It involves relationship. Voldemort considers it stupid to think that there is safety in relationship.[107] Weakness is involved. Yet it is precisely weakness—weakness that is open to the other and so forges bonds of trust and relationship—that defeats Voldemort's power. It is highly significant that the next time Harry faces Voldemort's Killing Curse, he is completely defenseless. His wand is stuffed beneath his robes, because he does not want to be tempted to fight.[108]

Weakness betters power: Voldemort comes out the worse from this encounter. The portion of his soul that he puts in Harry, when he accidentally makes him a Horcrux, is dispatched to a whimpering existence in the next world.[109] Voldemort himself, it seems, collapses and falls unconscious.[110] Although this also happens to Harry, it gives him a vision of what is beyond death as well as the confidence to face Voldemort as the latter again uses the Killing Curse on him.[111] Harry's willingness to go defenseless to his death for the sake of others gives them protection against Voldemort's spells.[112] Voldemort describes this to his followers as a "weakness,"[113] but it overcomes his power. In fact, Voldemort's power is what weakens him. It is precisely the exercise of his power that makes Harry—and others—into enemies. Dumbledore explains the dynamic of this to Harry:

> "If Voldemort had never murdered your father, would he have imparted in you a furious desire for revenge? Of course not! If he had not forced your mother to die for you, would he have given you a magical protection he could not penetrate? Of course not, Harry! Don't you see? Voldemort himself created his worst enemy, just as tyrants everywhere do! Have you any idea how much tyrants fear the people they oppress? All of them realize that, one day, amongst their many victims, there is sure to be one who rises against them and strikes back! Voldemort is no different!"[114]

It is this power, weakened by itself and by the willing weakness of its opponents, that Harry finally confronts in the Great Hall. He does this with his own signature spell. It is a spell Hogwarts considers suitable for second-year students. This is the spell that he has learned from Snape using it on Lockhart,[115] and has himself used on Lockhart.[116] Its apparent weakness is emphasized when he ineffectually uses it with a broken wand.[117] Yet it defeats Voldemort. When the two spells that confronted each other in the graveyard confront each other once more, this time in the Great Hall, Harry does indeed expel from the world the will for death in the person of Voldemort.[118] Evil power is turned against itself. *Expelliarmus* in its weakness is stronger than *Avada Kedavra* in its strength. The words of the psalmist are proved true: "Their mischief returns upon their own heads, / and on their own heads their violence descends."[119] Voldemort's final repetition of his initial mistake of using the Killing Curse on Harry is fatal to himself.[120] The boy who lived becomes the man who lived;[121] or, in the words that scripture attributes to the Lord of Life, he is "the living one."[122]

NOT WORSHIPPING POWER

Of course Harry is not the only one who fights Lord Voldemort. Others do too, and their strength also is that they do not make an absolute of power. Their measured abstinence from the wielding of power, an apparent weakness, is in a sense their strength: it enables them to gain respect and influence others. Dumbledore, says Professor McGonagall, is too "noble" to use power like Voldemort.[123] Harry makes a similar point in his final dialogue with Voldemort, who blindly dismisses it as meaning that Dumbledore is "weak."[124] Moody never kills if he can help it.[125] This echoes the Christian teaching about the Lord of Life: that he is omnipotent, but does not use his power to defend himself when he is attacked by his enemies. When they come to arrest Jesus, he tells one of his followers to put his sword back into its place, commenting, "Do you think that I cannot appeal to my Father, and he will at once send me more than twelve legions of angels?"[126] Dumbledore on the lightning-struck tower is like this. Harry, like the follower of Jesus drawing his sword,[127] draws his wand and Dumbledore wordlessly immobilizes him.[128] This he does at his own cost: the second he takes to perform the spell costs him the chance of defending himself.[129]

The interview with Draco Malfoy that follows echoes that between Jesus and Pilate, as recorded in chapter 19 of Saint John's Gospel. Pilate thinks he is the one with power, but he is told he would not have it unless it had been given to him from above.[130] Draco thinks he has power over Dumbledore, but the latter shows no sign of panic or distress. He responds to the news that Death Eaters are in his school "as though Malfoy was showing him an ambitious homework project," and talks "conversationally" and "kindly" to him.[131] In fact, Dumbledore is intending to die. This parallels what Jesus said of his own life: "No one takes it from me, but I lay it down of my own accord."[132] Both deaths have a purpose beyond that which others understand. Dumbledore is not exactly dying to redeem the world, but he does intend to empower Snape to rid the world of the death-dealing Voldemort. He does this by giving Snape a cover that will make him unsuspected by Voldemort, to whom the killing of Dumbledore will be evidence of Snape's allegiance. Dumbledore also offers mercy.

When Malfoy says to him, "You're in my power....I'm the one with the wand....You're at my mercy...," Dumbledore responds quietly, "No, Draco....It is my mercy, and not yours, that matters now."[133] This parallels Pilate's question to Christ, "Do you not know that I have power to release you, and power to crucify you?"[134] The Christian understanding is that this power, and thus its mercy, is God's, and Jesus shows that mercy to the world—and to Pilate—by dying to save both.[135]

There is another episode in which Dumbledore's behavior seems to reflect that of Jesus when under threat. It is when Dumbledore disappears from his enemies with a flash of fire, grasping the tail of his phoenix.[136] This recalls when Jesus angers "all in the synagogue." They want to hurl him off the cliff on which the town is built, but he passes amid them untouched and goes on his way.[137] The synagogue represents the religious authority of Jesus' day; and Fudge, who is trying to have Dumbledore captured, represents the magical authority of his day. The phoenix is also a link between Dumbledore and the Lord of Life: it is the bird of the resurrection.

Dumbledore does not, however, have a straightforward relationship with power. If he can in some respects be compared with the One who said, "Learn from me; for I am gentle and humble in heart,"[138] he has also struggled with the temptation to abuse power. Like the warlock with the hairy heart in *The Tales of Beedle the Bard*, he has known "one of the greatest, and least acknowledged, temptations of magic: the quest for invulnerability."[139] In the correspondence of his youth with Gellert Grindelwald, he is in favor of wizards dominating Muggles for their own good and seizing control "for the greater good."[140] This, of course, is like "the new world" that Voldemort wants to build.[141] Dumbledore is drawn by the lure of the Hallows. He seeks a way to conquer death, although, as Harry points out, he never kills if he can avoid it and, unlike Voldemort, he seeks the way through Hallows not Horcruxes.[142] Furthermore, he is self-aware enough to realize he is not to be trusted with power and repeatedly refuses the post of Minister of Magic.[143]

Like the quest in *The Lord of the Rings* to cast the one ring that rules them all into the fires of Mordor, the struggle to resist the lure of power is not easy. Dumbledore speaks of power as his weakness and temptation.[144] This shows real spiritual understanding. It is the perception that underlies the Rule of Saint Benedict, which offers a spiritual path of giving up one's own will and choosing to obey another's. It leads Dumbledore to refer to the Elder Wand, which he wins,[145] as "the meanest...the least extraordinary" Hallow.[146] It is an awareness that is utterly lacking in Voldemort, who thinks of his power not as his weakness, but as his strength. Dumbledore's struggle to move away from the unwisdom of the ignorance that characterizes Voldemort shows that Saint Paul's lesson, "Power is made perfect in weakness,"[147] is not easily learned. That Harry learns it so fully shows him to be an outstanding pupil of Hogwarts. His story is a school story, a story about learning, and this is a key part of what he learns.

The culmination of Harry's learning is his renunciation of the Elder Wand. This goes beyond what Dumbledore himself reaches. He shows the truth of Dumbledore's words to him:

> "Perhaps those who are best suited to power are those who have never sought it. Those who, like you, have leadership thrust upon them, and take up the mantle because they must, and find to their own surprise that they wear it well."[148]

Harry shows he is suited to power by not being addicted to it. He prefers destroying Horcruxes to going after the Elder Wand.[149] In refusing to go after the Elder Wand, Harry lays down power—leaving the wand in Voldemort's hands—and this, precisely, is his triumph. Like Jesus laying down his life, like Frodo taking the one ring that rules them all to the fires of Mordor, Harry lets the power to control others take second place to his mission. Harry does not become evil, but lets evil destroy itself. Taken from Voldemort, the Elder

Wand would not rebound the Killing Curse on him. Harry is a true Seeker—he knows how to resist the lust for power—and so the Elder Wand comes to him almost as a side effect of his battle against Voldemort and his Horcruxes.[150]

By this point his wisdom is such that his only use for it is to enable him to do without it. With it he mends his own wand,[151] whose loss left him feeling "fatally weakened, vulnerable and naked."[152] He then transcends the "desire for the Elder Wand, the Deathstick, unbeatable, invincible," which had once swallowed him.[153] He tells the portrait of Dumbledore, who is "watching him with enormous affection and admiration," that he is putting the wand back in his tomb.[154] This final renunciation goes beyond the achievement of defeating Voldemort. Harry explains what it achieves:

> "If I die a natural death like Ignotus, its power will be broken, won't it? The previous master will never have been defeated. That'll be the end of it."[155]

By his willingness to die, Harry has defeated Voldemort. By his actual death, he will defeat the Elder Wand, the cause of so much strife and bloodshed. The sacrifice of not using it is to be completed by his final letting go of this life. It is a sacrifice that fulfils the destiny he was given when his mother sacrificed her own life to save his: it is a sacrifice that returns the love that his mother showed in giving her life. And the love has become a love for all wizardkind.

The ability to choose weakness over power is a capacity for sacrifice, and that sacrifice is love in action. To be weak is to be open to another, to enter relationship. Sacrifice is accepting the weakness of loss, even loss of life, for the

good of others. It is the fountain of love. The next chapter
explores JK's presentation of this theme of love and sacrifice.

Notes

1. *The Philosopher's Stone*, chapter 1.
2. *The Deathly Hallows*, 562–64.
3. *The Deathly Hallows*, 596.
4. *The Philosopher's Stone*, 8.
5. *The Deathly Hallows*, 596.
6. *The Philosopher's Stone*, 15.
7. *The Philosopher's Stone*, 15.
8. *The Goblet of Fire*, 566.
9. *The Deathly Hallows*, 591.
10. Matthew 2:13–18.
11. *The Philosopher's Stone*, 15.
12. *The Deathly Hallows*, 595.
13. 1 Corinthians 1:25.
14. Revelation 5:5–6.
15. 1 Corinthians 1:25.
16. Isaiah 53:7.
17. *The Philosopher's Stone*, 47.
18. *The Half-Blood Prince*, 522–23.
19. *The Philosopher's Stone*, 45.
20. Isaiah 53:5.
21. *The Philosopher's Stone*, 71.
22. John 20:25.
23. *The Philosopher's Stone*, chapter 17.
24. *The Deathly Hallows*, 607.
25. *The Deathly Hallows*, 308.
26. 2 Corinthians 12:8.
27. 2 Corinthians 12:10.
28. *The Prisoner of Azkaban*, 275.
29. *The Prisoner of Azkaban*, 279.

30. *The Prisoner of Azkaban*, 310–11.
31. *The Prisoner of Azkaban*, 311.
32. Luke 23:34.
33. *The Order of the Phoenix*, 743.
34. Song of Solomon 8:6–7.
35. 2 Corinthians 12:8.
36. *The Deathly Hallows*, 380.
37. *The Deathly Hallows*, 380–81.
38. *The Order of the Phoenix*, 348.
39. *The Goblet of Fire*, 605.
40. *The Goblet of Fire*, 577–79.
41. *The Prisoner of Azkaban*, 279.
42. 1 John 4:16.
43. John 4:7.
44. Song of Solomon 8:6.
45. *The Deathly Hallows*, 55.
46. *The Deathly Hallows*, 56.
47. *The Deathly Hallows*, 63–64.
48. *The Chamber of Secrets*, 250.
49. *The Goblet of Fire*, 548.
50. *The Half-Blood Prince*, 250.
51. *The Deathly Hallows*, 282.
52. *The Half-Blood Prince*, 488.
53. *The Half-Blood Prince*, 546–53.
54. *The Half-Blood Prince*, 546.
55. *The Philosopher's Stone*, 216–17.
56. *The Deathly Hallows*, 307.
57. *The Philosopher's Stone*, 127.
58. *The Philosopher's Stone*, 219.
59. *The Order of the Phoenix*, 763.
60. *The Half-Blood Prince*, 599.
61. *The Half-Blood Prince*, 602.
62. *The Deathly Hallows*, 99.
63. *The Deathly Hallows*, 587.

64. *The Deathly Hallows*, 159.
65. *The Deathly Hallows*, 198–99.
66. *The Deathly Hallows*, 568.
67. *The Order of the Phoenix*, 118.
68. *The Order of the Phoenix*, 117.
69. *The Order of the Phoenix*, 118.
70. *The Philosopher's Stone*, 211.
71. *The Philosopher's Stone*, 211.
72. *The Goblet of Fire*, 567.
73. *The Philosopher's Stone*, 216.
74. *The Deathly Hallows*, 527.
75. *The Goblet of Fire*, 108.
76. *The Deathly Hallows*, 379.
77. *The Philosopher's Stone*, 204–5.
78. *The Deathly Hallows*, 161–64.
79. *The Philosopher's Stone*, 216.
80. *The Goblet of Fire*, 569.
81. *The Goblet of Fire*, 558.
82. *The Goblet of Fire*, 567.
83. *The Deathly Hallows*, 350.
84. *The Chamber of Secrets*, 12.
85. *The Goblet of Fire*, chapter 14.
86. *The Goblet of Fire*, 570.
87. *The Goblet of Fire*, 571.
88. *The Deathly Hallows*, 171.
89. *The Goblet of Fire*, 190.
90. Revelation 20:14.
91. *The Deathly Hallows*, 64.
92. *The Goblet of Fire*, 562.
93. *The Philosopher's Stone*, 15.
94. *The Goblet of Fire*, 570 and 573.
95. *The Goblet of Fire*, 605.
96. *The Goblet of Fire*, 575.
97. *The Goblet of Fire*, 580.

98. *The Deathly Hallows*, 596.
99. *The Order of the Phoenix*, 717.
100. *The Order of the Phoenix*, 715.
101. *The Order of the Phoenix*, 118.
102. *The Order of the Phoenix*, 186–87.
103. *The Goblet of Fire*, 627.
104. *The Order of the Phoenix*, 117.
105. *The Deathly Hallows*, 586.
106. *The Goblet of Fire*, 627.
107. *The Deathly Hallows*, 281.
108. *The Deathly Hallows*, 563.
109. *The Deathly Hallows*, 565 and 568.
110. *The Deathly Hallows*, 581.
111. *The Deathly Hallows*, chapter 35.
112. *The Deathly Hallows*, 591.
113. *The Deathly Hallows*, 525.
114. *The Half-Blood Prince*, 476–77.
115. *The Chamber of Secrets*, 142.
116. *The Chamber of Secrets*, 220.
117. *The Order of the Phoenix*, 285.
118. *The Deathly Hallows*, 595–96.
119. Psalm 7:16.
120. *The Deathly Hallows*, 596.
121. *The Philosopher's Stone*, chapter 1.
122. Revelation 1:18.
123. *The Philosopher's Stone*, 14.
124. *The Deathly Hallows*, 592.
125. *The Goblet of Fire*, 462.
126. Matthew 26:52–53.
127. Matthew 26:51.
128. *The Half-Blood Prince*, 545.
129. *The Half-Blood Prince*, 546.
130. John 19:11.
131. *The Half-Blood Prince*, 546–47.

132. John 10:18.

133. *The Half-Blood Prince*, 553.

134. John 19:10.

135. John 3:16.

136. *The Order of the Phoenix*, 549.

137. Luke 4:28–30.

138. Matthew 11:29.

139. J. K. Rowling, *The Tales of Beedle the Bard* (London: Children's High Level Group, 2008), 56.

140. *The Deathly Hallows*, 291.

141. *The Deathly Hallows*, 584.

142. *The Deathly Hallows*, 571.

143. *The Deathly Hallows*, 575.

144. *The Deathly Hallows*, 575.

145. *The Deathly Hallows*, 575.

146. *The Deathly Hallows*, 576.

147. 2 Corinthians 12:8.

148. *The Deathly Hallows*, 575.

149. *The Deathly Hallows*, 392.

150. *The Deathly Hallows*, 595–96.

151. *The Deathly Hallows*, 599.

152. *The Deathly Hallows*, 286.

153. *The Deathly Hallows*, 353.

154. *The Deathly Hallows*, 600.

155. *The Deathly Hallows*, 600.

6

To Lay Down One's Life for One's Friends

LOVE AND SACRIFICE

"It is impossible to manufacture or imitate love," says Professor Slughorn in a Potions lesson, distinguishing love from "a powerful infatuation or obsession."[1] This chapter is not about the sort of thing that happens when someone eats Chocolate Cauldrons spiked with a love potion, as Ron does, leading him to an intense but brief infatuation with Romilda Vane.[2] That is not real love. As a footnote in *The Tales of Beedle the Bard* tells us, "Powerful infatuations can be induced by the skilful potioneer, but never yet has anyone managed to create the truly unbreakable, eternal, unconditional attachment that alone can be called Love."[3] However, *pace* Hector Dagworth-Granger,[4] it is not only attachment that can be called love. Real love is not confined to romantic love. Love is present whenever someone acts with disinterested care for another. Love in this sense is what this chapter explores. Above all, it focuses on love that costs something: love that involves sacrifice. This by no means excludes romantic love, but this chapter will emphasize the love that characterizes every positive effort in favor of others. This is a love that gives despite the interests of the self.

RON'S SACRIFICES

Ron is a good exemplar of this love. He is not associated with self-denial in matters of food: when Hermione pushes away hers in protest at the lack of remuneration for house-elves, he tells her, "You won't get them sick leave by starving yourself!"[5] But he explicitly sacrifices himself in his first year at Hogwarts. When he, Harry, and Hermione are on a quest to stop the Philosopher's Stone from falling into evil hands, Ron, a skilled chess player,[6] masterminds a game of chess to get past an enchantment barring access to it. He becomes a knight. He soon shows chivalric values. "Yes," he says, "it's the only way—I've got to be taken." He does this in the full knowledge that the other side is showing "no mercy." His fellow knight has been smashed to the floor and dragged off the board, to lie quite still, face down.

When Harry and Hermione shout, "NO!" Ron responds, "That's chess!…You've got to make some sacrifices!"[7] And to stop the stone falling into the wrong hands (not Snape's hands, as he imagines[8]—in fact, hands that are literally allergic to love),[9] Ron allows himself to be struck hard around the head by the stone arm of the queen and dragged to one side. This enables Harry to checkmate the opposing king, and thus he and Hermione can get through to the next defense of the stone.[10] Ron shows himself consistent in his willingness to offer himself in sacrifice. In the final book, when Hermione is to be tortured before being handed over to the evil and predatory werewolf Greyback, he offers himself in her place, saying, "You can have me, keep me!"[11] This is no transitory and vain love, like that he felt for Romilda: this is the real thing. Although, of course, Ron is romantically linked with Hermione, this is a love that participates in the truest friendship, that of being willing to lay down one's life for one's friends.[12]

LEARNING TO SACRIFICE

This love, the love that Jesus taught and exemplified, is a key value in the Harry Potter series. The story begins and ends with this love. Ron's willingness to sacrifice himself for Hermione is a mature version of his sacrifice in chess. What in the first year he learns in the course of a game, in his last year he enacts in his life. It is not just Ron's exemplification of love that begins and ends the story. In the very first chapter we are told of the death of Harry's mother.[13] She sacrifices her life out of love for him. At the end of the final book, Harry goes willingly to his death to stop others from being killed.[14] He proves that "his deepest nature is…like his mother's."[15] He has learned to act as she does.

The entire series is about learning, and—as he learned about power and weakness—Harry also learns about sacrifice. What to Voldemort is a "woman's foolish sacrifice"[16] is the lesson expounded by Dumbledore. Voldemort gives Harry the facts. "Your mother needn't have died," he says. "She was trying to protect you."[17] Dumbledore interprets the facts; his explanation, which moves Harry to tears,[18] is in a sense the hermeneutic key to the whole series. It sets before Harry—and the reader—the contrast between the deep wisdom of love (typified by Lily Potter's sacrifice) and a deep ignorance of love (typified by Voldemort's and Quirrell's refusal of it). Dumbledore says:

"Your mother died to save you. If there is one thing Voldemort cannot understand, it is love. He didn't realize that love as powerful as your mother's for you leaves its own mark. Not a scar, no visible sign....To have been loved so deeply, even though the person who loved us is gone, will give us some protection for ever. It is in your very skin. Quirrell, full of hatred, greed, and ambition, sharing his soul with Voldemort, could not touch you for this reason. It was agony to touch a person marked by something so good."[19]

THE AGONY OF REFUSING LOVE

The essential weakness of those who have not learned this lesson is illustrated by Quirrell's inability to touch Harry's bare skin "without suffering terrible pain." When Quirrell's hand closes on Harry's wrist, his fingers blister before his eyes and he howls with agony. When Harry grabs his face, this too blisters.[20] JK has found in this blistering an "objective correlative" (to use T. S. Eliot's phrase) for the pain that those committed to evil feel in the presence of good. A prisoner, who had been involved in devil worship, spoke to me of this. Mentioning a particular church in London, he said that those who took part in satanic ritual could not enter it. They would be prostrated by goodness. This, he said, would be the case for any church in which there was sincere worship or fellowship. He was saying, in effect, that those committed to evil could not tolerate love. This is exactly what JK is dramatizing in making Quirrell unable to touch Harry's skin. We could take this understanding further and say that what Quirrell—and the Satan worshippers—experience is a foretaste of hell. God, the Bible says, is love.[21] He loves everyone with perfect love.

That some experience the fullness of bliss after this life and that some suffer is not due to the fact that God treats them differently. He treats them all the same. He loves them. It is just that for some, like Quirrell and Voldemort, love is painful to bear. This explains why Voldemort finds it so painful when he tries to take over Harry's body during the struggle in the Atrium in the Ministry of Magic (toward the end of the fifth book) in the hope of luring Dumbledore into killing Harry.[22] Harry, whose scar makes him sensitive to Voldemort's feelings and thoughts, feels this agony, "every part of him screaming for release."[23] It is the power of love that produces this feeling in Voldemort.

In a reprise of the lesson he taught Harry about Quirrell's inability to touch him, Dumbledore explains to him that this same power has saved him from possession by Voldemort, "because he could not bear to reside in a body so full of the force he detests."[24] He comments about this to Snape: "It was pain such as he has never experienced. He will not try to possess Harry again, I am sure of it." When Snape doesn't understand, he explains, "Lord Voldemort's soul, maimed as it is, cannot bear close contact with a soul like Harry's."[25] Love is integrity: a closeness to God, in whom there is perfect oneness, a willingness to share his loving embrace of all he has made. Evil is wanting selfish advantage at the expense of others. The two cannot coexist.

When Voldemort's integrity, repeatedly torn by the murderous creation of Horcruxes, meets Harry's integrity, the latter's unifying force goes painfully against the current of his shallow being. The one who has depended on scattering his soul in the world to maintain his illusion of immortality finds his soul being drawn away from its multiple hiding places to a center that he dares not trust. To him, with his low view of what constitutes life, this is the approach of death, and he experiences it as a death agony.

LOVE'S DEFEAT OF VOLDEMORT

In a sense, love is the death of Voldemort. It is not that his death is wished as such—indeed, Harry invites him to the path of life by advising him to "try for some remorse"[26]—rather, it is Harry's love that leads him to be willing to sacrifice himself, with fatal consequences for Voldemort. Harry leaves himself open to attack and that attack rebounds on the attacker.[27] This is, of course, an echo of the attack on baby Harry, when his mother's love leads her to be willing to sacrifice herself for him; because of this sacrifice, the curse rebounds on Voldemort and he is ripped from his body.[28] However, although love first weakens and then is the death of Voldemort, we can say that it is not so much a source of death but rather an end of death. This is because Voldemort—as his name implies—is the One Who Wants Death. To his defeat can be applied Shakespeare's line, "Death once dead, there's no more dying then."[29]

In destroying Voldemort, source of death, love shows itself indeed to be as strong as death.[30] Harry's love destroys Voldemort, in an echo and imitation of his mother's love, which destroyed Quirrell. The latter is left to die by Voldemort after he is unable to harm Harry, thanks to his mother's sacrifice.[31] This sacrifice also stops Harry from dying. Referring to the spell in which Voldemort took "Flesh, Blood, and Bone" to reincarnate himself,[32] Dumbledore explains:

> "He took your blood believing it would strengthen him. He took into his body a tiny part of the enchantment your mother laid upon you when she died for you. His body keeps her sacrifice alive, and while that enchantment survives, so do you."[33]

Dumbledore speculates that this taking of Harry's blood also increased Harry's power in the wand-to-wand struggle with Voldemort in the graveyard. He sees it as Voldemort's taking into himself, not just Harry's blood, but part of his mother's sacrifice. Dumbledore comments:

> "If he could only have understood the precise and terrible power of that sacrifice, he would not, perhaps, have dared to touch your blood."[34]

THE POWER OF SACRIFICE, ESPECIALLY LILY'S

Dumbledore knows the power of this sacrifice in a way Voldemort does not. He uses it to protect Harry. He uses a defensive move that is painful for Harry, like Dobby's rogue Bludger,[35] but more effective. He puts his trust in Harry's mother's blood, and delivers him "to her sister, her only remaining relative." That way, Harry is protected from Voldemort "by an ancient magic of which he knows, which he despises, and which he has always, therefore, underestimated—to his cost." Dumbledore is speaking, of course, of the fact that Harry's mother died to save him. He tells him, "She gave you a lingering protection he never expected, a protection that flows in your veins to this day."[36] "This is old magic," says Voldemort, admitting he has overlooked it.[37]

This ancient magic echoes that which is associated with the death of Aslan in C. S. Lewis's *The Lion, the Witch, and the Wardrobe*. It can also be taken to allude, as does Lewis's story, to the ancient Christian tradition that the power in the sacrifice of Christ is a protection against evil—hence, the practice of using a crucifix in exorcism. The same allusion is present when Dumbledore explains his decision to place

Harry in the care of his aunt, saying, "Your mother's sacrifice made the bond of blood the strongest shield I could give you."[38] Living with his aunt shields Harry from Voldemort and his Death Eaters; this is redolent of the belief that taking refuge in Jesus' blood shields Christians from evil. The language in which Dumbledore explains this shield echoes the language of Christian hymns about the blood of Jesus:

> "While you can still call home the place where your mother's blood dwells, there you cannot be touched or harmed by Voldemort. He shed her blood, but it lives on in you and her sister. Her blood became your refuge."[39]

The blood of Jesus, as received in holy communion, is called "the precious blood." This is a reference to both the value of the one who died and the value of his sacrifice, not least in the protection it gives from evil. The sacrifice of Lily Potter reflects this value, and the exploration of it through this fiction illuminates it. Even Voldemort, though underestimating it, has to acknowledge the power of her sacrifice, like the devil acknowledging the power of Christ's sacrifice. "His mother died in the attempt to save him—and unwittingly provided him with a protection," he says. And he understands where that protection comes from. "His mother left upon him the traces of her sacrifice," he explains.[40] But his knowledge, as Dumbledore says, remains "woefully incomplete." Voldemort does not understand that, because of "Lily's protection,"[41] when he takes Harry's blood, he is tethering Harry to life while he himself lives. In the movie of the sixth book, Harry's blood is called "precious."

In the blindness of his selfishness, Voldemort does not understand the depth and wisdom of Lily's unselfishness. Furthermore, there is no reason to suppose that he is necessarily correct in thinking that Lily did not understand the effect of her sacrifice. Certainly he did not understand the effect of his attack. This is reminiscent of Saint Gregory the Great's explanation of how Christ defeated the devil on Calvary: Christ's humanity was the bait which the devil took: his godhead was the hook that caught him. Lily's weakness is the bait that Voldemort took: her love is the hook that catches him. God is love.[42] Love catches Voldemort. It saves Harry, and Voldemort's battle against Harry kills him when his curse again rebounds.[43] "God so loved the world that he gave his only Son, so that everyone who believes in him may not perish but may have eternal life."[44] Love is his meaning, and that love, the Christian faith teaches us, snatches us from the evil that the devil would ensnare us in. The means of that rescue is sacrifice, the sacrifice of the cross. Lily Potter echoes this sacrifice.

Her sacrifice is, of course, not the only sacrifice in the series that echoes the cross. Indeed, it cannot be that any one character can take the place of Christ, since the depiction of God's own work is beyond fiction, even that of the most imaginative mind. Fiction can reflect what is done by showing characters that follow in Christ's footsteps: moons, as it were, reflecting the light of his sun. These are not perfect characters—even Lily, who is a pretty untarnished example for Harry, is implicated in reading her sister's private correspondence[45]—but they show something of the light of Christ in the sacrifice they make. And because one character alone cannot show the whole thing, it is appropriate that the tangential depiction of Christ's sacrifice should be refracted through multiple characters, each, as it were, displaying an aspect of it.

DUMBLEDORE'S SACRIFICE

Dumbledore is one such character. In a sense, like Lily, he dies to save Harry. He immobilizes him to stop him from getting involved in fighting the Death Eaters. This involvement would have betrayed Harry's presence under the Invisibility Cloak and made him a target. But the second that Dumbledore takes to perform this spell costs him the chance of defending himself.[46] However, as with Harry's own sacrifice (or, at least, his intention), Dumbledore is also sacrificially involved in the defeat of Voldemort's evil, mirroring the defeat of the devil. This is perhaps at its clearest in the episode that reflects the prayer of Christ in the Garden of Gethsemane: "Father, if you are willing, remove this cup from me; yet not my will but yours be done."[47]

In this episode Dumbledore literally drains a cup as part of his larger quest to prevent Voldemort from acting in the world; his immediate quest is to find a Horcrux. Dumbledore finds a stone basin, which is on a pedestal in the middle of a lake in a cave. In the basin is an emerald liquid emitting a phosphorescent glow. He says, "I can only conclude that this potion is supposed to be drunk" and conjures a crystal goblet out of the air. He explains, "Only by drinking it can I empty the basin and see what lies in its depths."[48] That this act is sacrificial is clear from what Dumbledore foresees about the way in which the potion might act to prevent him taking the Horcrux. "It might," he says, "paralyze me, cause me to forget what I am here for, create so much pain that I am distracted, or render me incapable in some other way."

He assigns Harry the job of making him drink it whatever his protests, echoing in a way the even less palatable job he has assigned to Snape—that of killing him.[49] And Dumbledore indeed drinks the cup he must drink, not once but eleven times. Like Christ in the Garden of Gethsemane, who is "deeply grieved, even to death,"[50] Dumbledore knows mortal anguish. He screams, "I want to die! I want to die!"[51] There is a hint too that Dumbledore—and Harry—share the experience of Christ that the Apostles' Creed refers to when it says, "He descended into hell." This is Dumbledore's descent among the dead. When he and Harry sail back across the lake, this scene meets them:

> The surface of the lake was no longer mirror-smooth; it was churning, and everywhere Harry looked, white heads and hands were emerging from the dark water, men and women and children with sunken, sightless eyes were moving towards the rock: an army of the dead rising from the black water.[52]

Together Dumbledore and Harry battle death in the form of the Inferi:[53] their very name suggests the infernal fate from which the Savior gives release. After they escape, Dumbledore says something that resonates with the story of the incarnation: "I am weak."[54] Coming from "the best wizard in the world,"[55] from the only one Voldemort ever feared,[56] this echoes the way Christ "emptied himself,"[57] knowing human weakness in thirst[58] and in sorrow.[59] Specifically, Dumbledore's croaking plea for water[60] recalls Christ's request to the Samaritan woman at the well: "Give me a drink."[61] This is also traditionally associated with his cry from the cross: "I am thirsty,"[62] which is interpreted to mean that he is thirsting for souls, for the salvation of humankind. Christ takes on the weakness of human flesh so that we can be saved by the strength of his divinity. Dumbledore, while—as has been said—obviously not sharing in the perfection of Christ's divinity, allows himself to experience weakness for a similar purpose: saving wizardkind (and Muggles) from the death-dealing evil of Voldemort. That he too is concerned with the salvation of souls is clear from a comment he makes to Harry, by way of encouraging him to return to life in the world so that he can defeat Voldemort. "By returning," he says, "you may ensure that fewer souls are maimed, fewer families are torn apart." He puts before him the motive of compassion for "those who live without love."[63]

It is reasonable to suppose that these motives are Dumbledore's own when he undergoes the weakness and the thirst that are the price he has to pay to reach the hiding place of what he believes to be a portion of Lord Voldemort's soul; also when he sheds his own blood to enter the cave where what he thinks is a Horcrux is hidden.[64] He is, in a sense, shedding his blood for the salvation of souls, after the pattern of Christ.

HARRY'S BAPTISM OF FIRE

A chapter is given to Dumbledore as his actions echo the Lord of Life drinking the cup in the Garden of Gethsemane.[65] A whole book is given to Harry when he does the same—*The Goblet of Fire*. Jesus asks his Father that the cup be removed from him; he asks of James and John: "Are you able to drink the cup that I am about to drink?"[66] When Harry's name is put into the Goblet of Fire, his ordeal evokes these other words from the Lord as well:

> "I came to bring fire upon the earth, and how I wish it were already kindled! I have a baptism with which to be baptized, and what stress I am under until it is completed!"[67]

The Lord's baptism is a baptism of fire. He accepts the cup he must drink in the Garden of Gethsemane and the result is the kindling of fire upon earth: the tongues of flame that descend upon the apostles at Pentecost.[68] Like the Lord of Life who prays, "If it is possible let this cup pass from me,"[69] Harry must accept the cup that he would rather not accept (he did not put his name in the Goblet of Fire).[70] He must be involved in the process that the fire demands of him. Like the Lord whose friends were not there for him in Gethsemane,[71] Harry knows the absence of the support of friendship: he and Ron fall out when Ron fails to believe that Harry did not put his own name in the cup.[72] Each of the three tasks that Harry has to undertake also in the Triwizard Tournament reflects in its own way the symbolism used in the gospels to convey the great work of suffering that the Lord Christ undertakes.

The first task is, indeed, a baptism of fire for him: he has to battle a Hungarian Horntail dragon, dodging the fire she breathes to take an egg from under her.[73] This echoes what is said above about the Lord's baptism of fire. The next task is a baptism by water: Harry has to go under the water to rescue his dearest friend.[74] Going under the water in baptism is a symbol of sharing the Lord's death. In Harry's case he risks actual death by his descent in the lake. The baptism with which the Lord is to be baptized is to save others. In Harry's descent under the lake, he saves not only his friend Ron, but also Fleur's sister, Gabrielle.[75] And he helps Krum rescue Hermione.[76] Echoing the Lord's prayerful acceptance in the garden of his cup of suffering,[77] Harry finally accepts a literal cup in his third task. He accepts the Triwizard Cup, which is bewitched to make it a Portkey that takes him to a deadly encounter with the evil Lord Voldemort. Unlike the Lord, who in accepting his cup of suffering confronts evil at the cost of his own death, Harry does not die, but Cedric does.[78] Cedric's death is a reminder of the cost of the struggle with evil, the price that was paid on Good Friday. It is an echo of the deaths of Christian martyrs.

Harry's baptism of fire is in Book 4, the central book of the series. It reflects the attack on him by Voldemort when he was a baby. The mark this leaves on his forehead[79] is redolent of the making of the sign of the cross on the forehead, which occurs during the baptism ceremony. At the same time the baptism of fire in Book 4 looks forward to Harry's undergoing (near) death (his visit to "King's Cross")[80] and his return to life in Book 7.[81] This is, in a sense, a sharing in the death and resurrection of Christ, which is what baptism is. The baptism of fire of Book 4 is central not only in structure but also in significance. It interprets the beginning and the end of the series. It invites us to make sense of the whole as a presentation of the baptizing of Harry: not in any merely formal sense, but in the sense of undergoing in his own person something of what Christ underwent in his passion, death, and resurrection. In this Harry learns the heart of values that are Christian.

In telling his story, JK is passing on these Christian values to her readers. She does this, not as one consciously deciding to be a spokeswoman for Christianity, but rather as one who is deeply imbued with the values of a civilization that has its roots in Christian history; as one who wants to pass these values to the next generation. The highest values of the culture come from the memory of Christ. To retell his story in the oblique kaleidoscope of fiction is to reassert those values.

Christ's story is not simply one of death and resurrection. It is also one of loneliness and misunderstanding. Christian tradition applies to Christ the words of the prophet Isaiah about the Suffering Servant: "He was despised and rejected by others."[82] Harry's central experience in the fourth book includes this rejection: not only does his best friend Ron abandon him, but others show that they despise him by magic badges displaying the glowing green legend, "*POTTER STINKS*."[83] Like Christ, Harry undergoes his baptism of fire in loneliness and misunderstanding. To his fellow pupils, his name being put in the goblet is simply a fast track to glory:[84] in reality, it is a plot by an unseen hand to draw him into the power of evil.[85]

Both Harry and Dumbledore have a cup to drink, as the Lord did in Gethsemane. They also each, in different ways, share in the Lord's death. Dumbledore dies literally; Harry goes to his death. Both of these are depicted in ways that link them to the death of Christ. As Christ dies on the cross to show mercy, so Dumbledore dies to show mercy: in particular, to Draco Malfoy. This is clear from his interview with Snape. He tells the latter, "Ultimately, of course, there is only one thing to be done if we are to save him from Lord Voldemort's wrath." When Snape asks sardonically, "Are you intending to let him kill you?" Dumbledore replies, "Certainly not. *You* must kill me."[86] Dumbledore dies so that Draco is not punished by Voldemort for his failure to kill him—a failure that Dumbledore accurately foresees.

HARRY'S SACRIFICES

The linking of Harry's going to his death with Christ's sacrifice is, if anything, even more explicit. After he has killed Voldemort, and the people in the Great Hall are rejoicing at his defeat and mourning their losses, Harry is described as "their savior." That he stands for something beyond himself is clear: "They wanted him there with them, their leader and symbol, their savior and their guide."[87] He is a symbol of what Christ has done. (In fact, the word *symbol* originally meant "creed.") And he leads and guides the others, and those who read the stories, by reflecting the values that come from the sacrifice of Christ. Other moments in the narrative reflect moments in the story of the Savior.

When Voldemort says, "Pick up your little friend, Hagrid,"[88] he is unconsciously creating a pietà: an icon of the dead Christ being held after he has been taken down from the cross. Hagrid is, of course, not an exact representation of the Virgin Mary, but he certainly partakes of her sorrow with "heaving sobs" and "great tears."[89] Harry's time in "King's Cross,"[90] where he meets Dumbledore—who matter-of-factly admits that he is dead[91]—corresponds to the descent to the dead of the Savior to which the Apostles' Creed refers, and which Holy Saturday commemorates.

If the mark that the infant Harry has received on his forehead[92] may be said to correspond to the sign of the cross, it is also an indication of what is accomplished on the cross: a direct confrontation with the power of evil. As well as being a symbol of Voldemort's first defeat,[93] it is the means by which Harry is linked to Voldemort. It gives him "dangerous access" to Voldemort's thoughts and feelings.[94] For example, it tells him when Voldemort is arriving for the battle of Hogwarts.[95] As a sign of Harry's link with Voldemort, it is also a sign of Voldemort's final downfall. In this context, it's described as being "like a bolt of lightning,"[96] which recalls the words of Jesus to his disciples returning from their mission: "I watched Satan fall from heaven like a flash of lightning."[97] Of course, the cross is above all a sign of sacrifice and Harry's story is a story of sacrifice.

The sacrifice that finally accomplishes the defeat of Voldemort is one of intention. Harry explains to Dumbledore, "I meant to let him kill me," and Dumbledore replies that this will "have made all the difference."[98] Intentions characteristically do not just suddenly appear. They are born of habits of mind and behavior. And so it is with Harry. He sacrifices time vital to victory in the second task of the Triwizard tournament "to return all hostages to safety, not merely his own."[99] The following year, when he becomes convinced that his link with Voldemort allows the latter to look "into the Headquarters of the Order of the Phoenix"[100] and so puts others at risk, he resolves "to return to Privet Drive, cut himself off from other wizards entirely."[101] Only a message from Dumbledore to stay where he is stops him from carrying out this resolution,[102] despite the fact that Hogwarts is his true home.[103]

In his sixth year at Hogwarts, Harry sacrifices his love for Ginny. He explains to her that they "can't be together" because "Voldemort uses people his enemies are close to."[104] This willingness to sacrifice is an indication of maturity. The first of these examples is in Harry's fourth year, narrated in the fourth book, which is the first of those that have an adult aspect. Each subsequent year, as we have seen, shows Harry willing to sacrifice. Even after his willingness to sacrifice his life to defeat Voldemort, Harry continues to behave in a sacrificial way. He resolves to put the Elder Wand "back where it came from" so that "its power will be broken."[105] This is the sacrifice of power, of the wand with the reputation for being unbeatable, whose value he has been aware of.[106] The whole series ends—in the epilogue—with another sacrifice: Harry cheerfully enduring "the little bereavement" of letting his young son go away for the first time to boarding school.[107] All of these sacrifices are preparations for, or reflections of, the resolve of mind that enables Harry to confront Voldemort with the willingness to sacrifice his own life.

This sacrifice is so central, both to the story and to Harry's conforming to Christ, that it merits examination in greater detail. It is the enactment of the saying of Christ, "I lay down my life in order to take it up again."[108] Harry knows this is "his true destiny."[109] He understands that he is "not supposed to survive."[110] As he walks to meet Voldemort, he knows the long game is ended, the Snitch has been caught, and it is time to leave the air.[111] He deliberately makes himself visible to Voldemort and loudly announces his presence.[112] He lays down his life. He sees "a flash of green light" and everything is gone.[113] Having talked with Dumbledore, who is dead, he takes his life up again, knowing that he is "heading back to pain and the fear of more loss." Even his return is a sacrifice, leaving a place where it is "warm and light and peaceful."[114] All of this sacrifice is for his friends, to prevent anyone else from dying.[115] He loves them.

Harry's sacrifice brings to mind this description of his feelings when members of the Order turn up at Number 4 Privet Drive:

> Harry's heart seemed to expand and glow at the sight: he felt incredibly fond of all of them, even Mundungus, whom he had tried to strangle last time they had met.[116]

It also recalls the words of Christ, "No one has greater love than this, to lay down one's life for one's friends."[117] Christ's sacrificial love also included a man who, like Mundungus, was a thief. He showed that his sacrifice included him by saying, "Truly I tell you, today you will be with me in Paradise."[118] The Lord's sacrifice, the Christian tradition teaches, sets us free from the dominion of evil. Harry's sacrifice has an analogous effect. He explains this to Voldemort, referring to the sacrifice from which he has benefited himself:

> "I've done what my mother did. They're protected from you. Haven't you noticed how none of the

spells you put on them are binding? You can't torture them. You can't touch them."[119]

This is shown by the way Neville is able to break free from the Body-Bind Curse to kill Nagini.[120] When Ron yells, "He beat you!" he also is benefiting from Harry's sacrifice, which has prevented Voldemort's Silencing Charm from holding.[121]

Harry beats Voldemort by sacrifice, which makes ironic his assessment of Harry as "a boy who relied on others to sacrifice themselves for him."[122] Harry does, of course, benefit from the sacrifice of others, particularly his mother's, which saves his life, but Voldemort misses—to the cost of his power—the fact that Harry has learned from this to sacrifice himself. "Don't you get it?" he says to Voldemort, "I was ready to die to stop you hurting these people."[123] The intention is sufficient, the same intention that his mother had when she sacrificed herself. At the end of the series, Voldemort, by contrast with Harry, has not understood "the precise and terrible power of that sacrifice."[124] He is justly taunted by Harry when he says, "You don't learn from your mistakes, Riddle, do you?"[125] Tom Riddle underestimates sacrifice to the very end.

OTHER CHARACTERS' SACRIFICE

In further contrast, plenty of other characters do see the value of sacrifice. Sirius Black puts himself in danger out of love for Harry (the person he cares most about in the world),[126] and consequently loses his life.[127] His relative Regulus Black sacrifices his life to diminish the power of Voldemort by taking one of his Horcruxes, writing a note for him saying, "I face death in the hope that when you meet your match, you will be mortal once more."[128] Severus Snape continually risks death by double-crossing Voldemort, and, even though his cover is not blown, he falls a sacrificial victim to the one "who shows just as little mercy to his followers as his enemies."[129] Remus Lupin, even though it means he will never know his son, dies "trying to make a world in which he could live a happier life."[130] Perhaps more obviously sacrificial than all of these is the death of Dobby. He comes "to save Harry Potter and his friends" and is killed by the evil woman he has confronted. His dying words— "Harry...Potter..."—express his love.[131]

The occasion of Dobby's death shows something of the power of love to counter Voldemort. Harry digs his grave, non-magically, "subsuming his grief in sweat," and finds that

> just as Voldemort had not been able to possess Harry while Harry was consumed with grief for Sirius, so his thoughts could not penetrate Harry now, while he mourned Dobby. Grief, it seemed, drove Voldemort out...though Dumbledore, of course, would have said that it was love.[132]

Grief, as Queen Elizabeth the Second said at a memorial service for those who died on 9/11, is the price we pay for love. It is the sacrifice implicit in love, and this sacrifice, this love, has power over evil. Evil cannot take possession of those whose grief is the sacrificial token of their love. Blessed are those who mourn, for they will be comforted.[133] The rage of Voldemort is dreadful, as he punishes those left behind at Malfoy Manor, yet Harry's grief for Dobby seems to diminish it, so that it becomes "a distant storm" that reaches Harry "from across a vast, silent ocean."[134] That ocean is love, which partakes of the vastness and silence of eternity.

LEARNING ABOUT LOVE

Harry receives a full teaching about this love from his Headmaster in his fifth and sixth years at Hogwarts. In his seventh, he shows himself to have assimilated it fully. When Harry is grieving intensely for Sirius, Dumbledore says to him, "The fact that you can feel pain like this is your greatest strength....Suffering like this proves you are still a man! This pain is part of being human." The pain is so intense that Harry retorts that he does not want to be human.[135] It is, in fact, a growing pain: Harry is growing in love. As with the grief about Dobby's death, this pain is a sign of his love, and so his humanity. In his adolescent pain, Harry smashes up Dumbledore's possessions, but the latter remains calmly detached.[136] Dumbledore insists on having his say[137] and interprets Harry's life, giving details of a prophecy made about him.[138] The prophecy says that Harry will have "*power the Dark Lord knows not.*"[139] This power is love. "Love is as strong as death,"[140] says scripture, and indeed this power is strong enough to stand up to Voldemort, the One Who Wants Death. Dumbledore explains the magic of love, showing how it is beyond Voldemort's understanding and reach. "There is a room in the Department of Mysteries," he says,

"that is kept locked at all times. It contains a force that is at once more wonderful and more terrible than death, than human intelligence, than the forces of nature. It is also, perhaps, the most mysterious of the many subjects for study that reside there. It is the power held within that room that you possess in such quantities and which Voldemort has not at all. That power took you to save Sirius tonight. That power also saved you from possession by Voldemort, because he could not bear to reside in a body so full of the force he detests. In the end, it mattered not that you could not close your mind. It was your heart that saved you."[141]

We see both the awesomeness and the attraction of this power in Ron's reaction to it when Hermione insists they leave the room that contains its force. He looks at the door that cannot be unlocked "with a mixture of apprehension and longing"[142]—a traditional response to the presence of the numinous. As was pointed out in the previous chapter, this power is, looked at from a certain point of view, weakness. It certainly seems so to Harry, who says he does not have any powers that Voldemort has not, meaning that he cannot fight as Voldemort fights, or possess people or kill them as he does.[143] In terms of what it leads to, it seems catastrophic: Voldemort lures Harry into danger, using the fact that Sirius Black is the one person he would go to any lengths to rescue.[144] With Harry in danger, Sirius does not wish to remain behind while others go to his aid.[145] The result is Sirius's death.[146]

Jesus met his death as a result of an active love, and the Friday on which it happened is called *good*. The opportunity to have him killed was taken by the devil as an opportunity for victory. Yet it was the moment of the devil's defeat, as he was brought into direct conflict with the divinity of Jesus. Similarly, Voldemort, in the fight in the Atrium of the Ministry of Magic, is brought into direct conflict—a conflict he loses—with the power of love. God is love, says Saint John.[147] And we know that all things work together for good to them that love God, says Saint Paul.[148] The good in Harry's story is not merely the defeat of Voldemort in the Atrium battle. Inwardly, it is Harry's painful growth in love. Outwardly, it is Voldemort's coming out into the open, which gives his opponents an advantage, relative to the time when his return was not widely believed. The Minister of Magic's statement that Voldemort has returned "and is once more active" marks an end to the division in the magical community about whether or not Voldemort is active.[149] This allows them more scope for coming together to fight him.

In his fifth year, Harry has come a long way in learning love and sacrifice. Just two years previously, he had been so oblivious to what his parents had done for him that he was "gambling their sacrifice for a bag of magic tricks."[150] The fourth year (Book 4) is the turning point in Harry's life: the point when things get serious. He changes from a schoolboy throwing mud at another schoolboy[151] to a youth witnessing the incarnation of evil.[152] The fifth year (Book 5) is that of adolescence. In it Harry feels pain, often expressed as anger. The pain is that of growth, growth in love. He is beginning to learn the connection between suffering and love. The sixth year (Book 6) sees him becoming more self-aware about his ability to love, and more aware of its importance. Dumbledore teaches him. He is the exegete of Harry's life: he makes sense of it for him. To Harry's protestation that he lacks the "uncommon skill and power" needed to kill a wizard like Voldemort, Dumbledore responds, "You have a power that Voldemort has never had." Harry remembers his lesson of the previous year well enough to be able to tell Dumbledore what this is—"I can love"—but does not fully understand how important this is. It is only with difficulty that he stops himself adding, "Big deal!" Emphasizing that the "power the Dark Lord knows not" is indeed "just love," Dumbledore points out to Harry that his ability to love is "a great and remarkable thing," given everything that has happened to him.[153] He tells Harry, "You are still too young to understand how unusual you are."

The unusualness is that Harry has "never been seduced by the Dark Arts." His love for his murdered parents is proof against that seduction. With a loudness that is so uncharacteristic it forcefully highlights the importance of the lesson he wants to get across, Dumbledore explains that Harry is protected by his ability to love. This is "the only protection that can possibly work against the lure of power like Voldemort's."[154] Only love can abjure power. Only love is strong enough to accept the weakness of not having power. Only love can outbid the offer of control made by evil. These are among the profoundly Christian lessons that Harry learns at Hogwarts.

He is being taught what Saint Paul taught: that power— the transcendent power of love—"is made perfect in weakness."[155] He is growing toward being big enough to forgo even the Elder Wand.[156] This is one of several indications in the seventh and final book that Harry has learned his lessons of love and sacrifice. Dumbledore's brother, Aberforth, insinuates that Dumbledore would have shown greater love for Harry if he had taught him how to take care of himself, how to survive, perhaps by hiding. Harry responds, "Sometimes you've *got* to think about the greater good!"[157] In other words, sacrifice can be necessary. By the time Harry is ready to graduate from Hogwarts, he is unwilling to let anyone else die for him, even at the cost of his own life, once he has discovered it is in his power to stop further killing.[158] He is schooled in sacrifice, and learned in love.

EXEMPLARS OF LOVE

In the series, there are plenty of exemplars of love who convey this value to Harry. As well as putting himself in danger for Harry, as already mentioned, Sirius Black does the more usual parental things as well, such as coming to watch him play sports (albeit in unusual form)[159] and giving him a Firebolt, an exceptionally generous Christmas present.[160] The strength of Harry's reaction to the loss of Sirius is a clear indication that he feels the value of this love.[161] Dumbledore loves Harry too. Indeed, by his own account, he does so to the point of weakness. "I cared about you too much," he tells Harry:

> "I cared more for your happiness than your knowing the truth, more for your peace of mind than my plan, more for your life than the lives that might be lost if the plan failed. In other words, I acted exactly as Voldemort expects we fools who love to act."[162]

He is referring to the truth of the prophecy about Harry and Voldemort,[163] which he did not want to burden him with.[164] Harry has many uncertainties about the reality of the love that Dumbledore has for him, but there is no doubt for the reader. From his murmured "Good luck, Harry"[165] to the little baby in the first chapter of the series, to his affirmation "You brave, brave man"[166] to the adult standing before him, Dumbledore shows—whatever his weaknesses—the love of a true educator for his pupil. Hermione (smart girl, that Hermione)[167] sees this clearly and is able to tell Harry, "He loved you, I know he loved you."[168]

Snape's love for Harry is even less obvious to him. Yet, although it cannot be said that Snape has friendly feelings toward him, the reality of Snape's actions indicate love. He protects Harry from Quirrell.[169] He tries to teach him Occlumency to protect him from having his thoughts and feelings accessed by Voldemort.[170] He passes onto the Order, on Harry's behalf, his concern about Voldemort and Sirius, and gives Umbridge fake Veritaserum when she attempts to force Harry to tell Sirius's whereabouts.[171] Snape's dying act is to give Harry the memories that he needs to fulfill his destiny; his dying look is into Harry's eyes that are so reminiscent of his mother's.[172] It might be a look of love. Snape has responded to Dumbledore's request, "Help me protect Lily's son,"[173] even though the care he has shown up to now has not been recognized by that son. By contrast, Harry has a more immediate awareness of the fiercely maternal love of Mrs. Weasley, who welcomes him to her home with eight or nine sausages and three fried eggs,[174] and hugs him after his terrible ordeal in the graveyard.[175] He has an example of love that sees beyond looks in Fleur's devotion to Bill.[176] Her radiance, on the day of her wedding, beautifies everyone upon whom it falls.[177] This is unselfish love.

Voldemort, Ignorant Enemy of Love

Unselfish love is presented both directly and by contrast. Voldemort, of course, provides the principal contrast. In a scene that exemplifies JK's genius for giving external form to spiritual realities, the Dark Lord kills Charity.[178] Charity Burbage is Muggle Studies teacher at Hogwarts. She writes in the *Daily Prophet* on behalf of those of Muggle origin.[179] She represents an understanding and inclusive approach to others. In a word, she symbolizes charity. In traditional Catholic moral theology, a mortal sin is said to be one that kills charity in the soul. The murder of Charity Burbage makes outwardly plain what is happening in Voldemort's soul. He is killing charity or love in his soul. As Dumbledore says, Voldemort understands nothing of love.[180] He values this supreme good so little that he acts to destroy it in himself. He becomes an enemy of love to the extent that its presence is an agony to him. Contact with it when he tries to possess Harry, who loves, is "pain such as he has never experienced."[181] This enmity toward love also leaves Voldemort irremediably obtuse. Shortly before he kills Charity, Voldemort says, "I understand those things that I did not understand before."[182]

Ironically, he never understands that which he has never understood: love. He remains in the same ignorance that Dumbledore identifies when he comes to Hogwarts asking for a job. On that occasion he claims the greatness of having "pushed the boundaries of magic further, perhaps, than they have ever been pushed." Dumbledore makes the correction that Voldemort has pushed the boundaries "of some kinds of magic," pointing out that he is "woefully ignorant" of others. Clearly this is an old argument, because Voldemort retorts, "Nothing I have seen in the world has supported your famous pronouncement that love is more powerful than my kind of magic." In reply Dumbledore simply suggests that Voldemort has been looking in the wrong places.[183] Since God is love,[184] this amounts to saying that Voldemort has been seeking God in the wrong places. It is reminiscent of Saint Augustine's words in his *Confessions*: "*Ecce intus eras et ego foris, et ibi te quaerebam.*"[185] (I quote in the original because I know JK's use of Latin has encouraged her readers to study it, but just in case it's Ancient Runes to you, this means, approximately, "Behold, you were within and I outside, and I was seeking you there.")

Like the young Augustine, Voldemort is very much an exterior person: living on the outside and seeking there. His putting of himself into Horcruxes is one indication of this exteriorization of his soul. Like the man in the parable who hides his talent in the ground,[186] Voldemort hides what he has been given: Dumbledore says, "The point of a Horcrux is…to keep part of the self hidden and safe."[187] Another indication of Voldemort's being an exterior person is his failure "to grasp that there are much more terrible things than physical injury," as Dumbledore remarks when he has to give blood to enter the cave where the Horcrux locket is hidden.[188] Voldemort never finds in his soul the "paradise within,"[189] the presence of God, who is love. This means that he remains always relatively weak, since God, as the Christian creed proclaims, is omnipotent. God, who is love, is almighty. Therefore, Voldemort, who is lacking in love, is lacking in power. He cannot share in ultimate power because he wants it just for himself. "He does not love."[190]

Dumbledore's dialogue with Voldemort about the latter's woeful ignorance of love is echoed in Harry's final dialogue with Voldemort. Using the name that his opponent had when a schoolboy, as if to emphasize his lack of real growth in understanding, he says, "I know things you don't know, Tom Riddle. I know lots of important things that you don't."[191] As with his dialogue with Dumbledore, Voldemort jeeringly rejects "Dumbledore's favorite solution, *love*, which he claimed conquered death." His argument is the argument of violence:

> "Love did not stop him falling from the Tower and breaking like an old waxwork. *Love* which did not prevent me stamping out your Mudblood mother like a cockroach, Potter—and nobody seems to love you enough to run forwards this time, and take my curse."[192]

Harry defends the wisdom of his teacher, and reveals to Voldemort what he doesn't know, precisely because of his ignorance of love: that Severus Snape was not his. "Snape was Dumbledore's," Harry tells him, "Dumbledore's from the moment you started hunting down my mother. And you never realized it, because of the thing you can't understand." He points out that, "Snape's Patronus was a doe…the same as my mother's because he loved her for nearly all of his life, from the time when they were children." Consequently, Voldemort is told, Snape "was Dumbledore's spy from the moment you threatened her, and he's been working against you ever since!"[193]

This is not the only way in which a failure to understand love works against Voldemort. As far as he can see, there is no reason why Narcissa Malfoy should not be on his side. He tells her to ascertain if Harry is dead after the encounter in the Forbidden Forest. Harry feels "hands softer than he had been expecting" examining him. Narcissa asks him in a whisper if her son is alive. When he answers in the affirmative, she lies to Voldemort that Harry is dead.[194] Harry understands why. "Narcissa knew that the only way she would be permitted to enter Hogwarts, and find her son, was as part of the conquering army. She no longer cared whether Voldemort won."[195] In other words, Voldemort has made the same mistake about Narcissa as he made about Snape: he has overlooked the possibility that they could be motivated by love. Narcissa loves her son, Draco. Finding him is, in the end, more important to her than Voldemort's cause. Voldemort loses out to love.

BELLATRIX, SOUL WITHOUT LOVE

Voldemort is not the only character who highlights the importance of love by contrast. Narcissa's sister, Bellatrix, does so also. It could be argued that she loves Voldemort. She screams, "MASTER!" when he disappears under the assault of Dumbledore's magic in the Atrium of the Ministry of Magic.[196] She interrogates Snape, whom she distrusts, to try to bring to light a suspected disloyalty to Voldemort.[197] She tells Voldemort that there can be "no higher pleasure" than to have him in the family house.[198] When Voldemort falls unconscious in the confrontation with Harry in the Forest, it is she who goes to help him.[199] However, for all this, there is no *relationship* between them.

When she has failed to get the prophecy and begs for Voldemort's mercy, he tells her to be quiet, saying, "Do you think I have entered the Ministry of Magic to hear your sniveling apologies?"[200] When she talks of her pleasure at having him in the family home, he humiliates her by drawing the attention of the Death Eaters to the marriage of her niece to "the werewolf, Remus Lupin," provoking "an eruption of jeering laughter" from those around the table.[201] When she tries to help him in the Forest, he says coldly, "I do not require assistance."[202] There is no love between them. Dumbledore is right to think that Voldemort has servants rather than friends.[203] In this he is the opposite of Jesus, who said, "I do not call you servants...but I have called you friends.[204]

Just as when he was a boy, the adult Voldemort is self-sufficient—and friendless. Those who think they are in relationship with him are deluded: he has never had a friend, and, Dumbledore thinks, has never wanted one.[205] It follows that love does not enter Bellatrix's soul through her encounter with Voldemort. Her true state is revealed in her ruthless reaction to her sister's distress about the mortal danger her son is in. "You should be proud," she says, and adds, rather in the manner of Shakespeare's Volumnia speaking about the defense of Rome,[206] "If I had sons, I would be glad to give them up to the service of the Dark Lord!"[207] She contrasts with her loving sister rather as Regan and Goneril, in Shakespeare's *King Lear*, contrast with Cordelia. Bellatrix is loveless to the point of not being able to love even her own, killing her cousin, Sirius Black.[208] She has no love for other people's children. She aims to kill Hermione, Ginny, and Luna, till she is defeated by Mrs. Weasley's true maternal love.[209] Like her master, she mocks love. After she has killed Sirius, she taunts Harry, "Aaaaaah…did you *love* him, little baby Potter?"[210]

THE TRIUMPH OF LOVE

Love, however, is triumphant. After the defeat of Voldemort, everywhere Harry looks in the Great Hall, he sees "families reunited."[211] The force "more wonderful and more terrible than death" wins.[212] The "somethin' goin'" on that night the infant Harry is first attacked is brought to its final conclusion: the sacrifice and love that save him leads to more love and sacrifice, which eventually see off the attacker.[213] The message that prevails is: "Pity…, above all, those who live without love."[214] This, of course, echoes Saint Paul's famous discourse about love, in which he wrote that if he had not love, he was nothing.[215]

There is more about love in the Harry Potter series than about anything else, and there is more to say about it here than what has already been said in this chapter. The idea that love, with its concomitant sacrifice, is a central value rests upon a particular understanding of the human person. It depends on the assumption that the human person is free to choose; that his or her behavior is not wholly determined by extrinsic factors. The next chapter looks at JK's treatment of this idea.

Notes

1. *The Half-Blood Prince*, 177.
2. *The Half-Blood Prince*, 366–71.

3. *The Tales of Beedle the Bard*, 58.
4. *The Tales of Beedle the Bard*, 58.
5. *The Goblet of Fire*, 162.
6. *The Goblet of Fire*, 354.
7. *The Philosopher's Stone*, 205.
8. *The Philosopher's Stone*, 205.
9. *The Philosopher's Stone*, 213.
10. *The Philosopher's Stone*, 206.
11. *The Deathly Hallows*, 375.
12. John 15:12–13.
13. *The Philosopher's Stone*, 14.
14. *The Deathly Hallows*, 555.
15. *The Deathly Hallows*, 549.
16. *The Goblet of Fire*, 566.
17. *The Philosopher's Stone*, 213.
18. *The Philosopher's Stone*, 217.
19. *The Philosopher's Stone*, 216.
20. *The Philosopher's Stone*, 213–14.
21. 1 John 4:16.
22. *The Order of the Phoenix*, 719–20 and 730.
23. *The Order of the Phoenix*, 719–20.
24. *The Order of the Phoenix*, 743.
25. *The Deathly Hallows*, 549.
26. *The Deathly Hallows*, 594.
27. *The Deathly Hallows*, 596.
28. *The Goblet of Fire*, 566.
29. Shakespeare, Sonnet 146, line 14.
30. Song of Solomon 8:6.
31. *The Philosopher's Stone*, 216.
32. *The Goblet of Fire*, chapter 32.
33. *The Deathly Hallows*, 568.
34. *The Deathly Hallows*, 569–70.
35. *The Chamber of Secrets*, chapter 10.
36. *The Order of the Phoenix*, 736.

37. *The Goblet of Fire*, 566.
38. *The Order of the Phoenix*, 737.
39. *The Order of the Phoenix*, 737.
40. *The Goblet of Fire*, 566.
41. *The Deathly Hallows*, 568.
42. 1 John 4:8.
43. *The Deathly Hallows*, 596.
44. John 3:16.
45. *The Deathly Hallows*, 537.
46. *The Half-Blood Prince*, 546.
47. Luke 22:42.
48. *The Half-Blood Prince*, 530–31.
49. *The Half-Blood Prince*, 532, and *The Deathly Hallows*, 548.
50. Matthew 26:38.
51. *The Half-Blood Prince*, 536.
52. *The Half-Blood Prince*, 537–38.
53. *The Half-Blood Prince*, 538–39.
54. *The Half-Blood Prince*, 540.
55. *The Philosopher's Stone*, 92.
56. *The Order of the Phoenix*, chapter 36.
57. Philippians 2:7.
58. John 4:7.
59. Matthew 26:38.
60. *The Half-Blood Prince*, 536.
61. John 4:10.
62. John 19:28.
63. *The Deathly Hallows*, 578.
64. *The Half-Blood Prince*, 523.
65. "The Cave," chapter 26 in *The Half-Blood Prince*.
66. Matthew 20:22.
67. Luke 12:49–50.
68. Acts 2:3.
69. Matthew 26:39.

70. *The Goblet of Fire*, 239.
71. Matthew 26:40.
72. *The Goblet of Fire*, 252.
73. *The Goblet of Fire*, 309–11.
74. *The Goblet of Fire*, chapter 26.
75. *The Goblet of Fire*, 435–37.
76. *The Goblet of Fire*, 434–35.
77. Matthew 26:39.
78. *The Goblet of Fire*, 551–53.
79. *The Philosopher's Stone*, 45.
80. *The Deathly Hallows*, 570.
81. *The Deathly Hallows*, 581 and 590.
82. Isaiah 53:3.
83. *The Goblet of Fire*, 261.
84. *The Goblet of Fire*, 260.
85. *The Goblet of Fire*, 587.
86. *The Deathly Hallows*, 548.
87. *The Deathly Hallows*, 596.
88. *The Deathly Hallows*, 582.
89. *The Deathly Hallows*, 582.
90. *The Deathly Hallows*, chapter 35.
91. *The Deathly Hallows*, 567.
92. *The Philosopher's Stone*, 45.
93. *The Philosopher's Stone*, 15.
94. *The Half-Blood Prince*, 61.
95. *The Deathly Hallows*, 488.
96. *The Philosopher's Stone*, 17.
97. Luke 10:18.
98. *The Deathly Hallows*, 567.
99. *The Goblet of Fire*, 440.
100. *The Order of the Phoenix*, 436.
101. *The Order of the Phoenix*, 437.
102. *The Order of the Phoenix*, 437–38.
103. *The Prisoner of Azkaban*, 74.

104. *The Half-Blood Prince*, 602.

105. *The Deathly Hallows*, 600.

106. *The Deathly Hallows*, 346.

107. *The Deathly Hallows*, 607.

108. John 10:17.

109. *The Deathly Hallows*, 556.

110. *The Deathly Hallows*, 554.

111. *The Deathly Hallows*, 559.

112. *The Deathly Hallows*, 563.

113. *The Deathly Hallows*, 564.

114. *The Deathly Hallows*, 579.

115. *The Deathly Hallows*, 555.

116. *The Deathly Hallows*, 44.

117. John 15:13.

118. Luke 23:43.

119. *The Deathly Hallows*, 591.

120. *The Deathly Hallows*, 587.

121. *The Deathly Hallows*, 585.

122. *The Deathly Hallows*, 585.

123. *The Deathly Hallows*, 591.

124. *The Deathly Hallows*, 569.

125. *The Deathly Hallows*, 591.

126. *The Order of the Phoenix*, 732.

127. *The Order of the Phoenix*, 711.

128. *The Half-Blood Prince*, 569.

129. *The Deathly Hallows*, 527–28, and *The Philosopher's Stone*, 216.

130. *The Deathly Hallows*, 561.

131. *The Deathly Hallows*, 384–85.

132. *The Deathly Hallows*, 387.

133. Matthew 5:4.

134. *The Deathly Hallows*, 386.

135. *The Order of the Phoenix*, 726.

136. *The Order of the Phoenix*, 726–27.

137. *The Order of the Phoenix*, 727.

138. *The Order of the Phoenix*, 735–44.

139. *The Order of the Phoenix*, 743.

140. Song of Solomon 8:6.

141. *The Order of the Phoenix*, 743.

142. *The Order of the Phoenix*, 684.

143. *The Order of the Phoenix*, 743.

144. *The Order of the Phoenix*, 733.

145. *The Order of the Phoenix*, 732.

146. *The Order of the Phoenix*, 711.

147. 1 John 4:16.

148. Romans 8:28 (King James Version).

149. *The Order of the Phoenix*, 745–46.

150. *The Prisoner of Azkaban*, 213.

151. *The Prisoner of Azkaban*, 207.

152. *The Goblet of Fire*, chapter 32.

153. *The Half-Blood Prince*, 476.

154. *The Half-Blood Prince*, 477.

155. 2 Corinthians 12:8.

156. *The Deathly Hallows*, 600.

157. *The Deathly Hallows*, 458.

158. *The Deathly Hallows*, 555.

159. *The Prisoner of Azkaban*, 133.

160. *The Prisoner of Azkaban*, 165 and 315.

161. *The Order of the Phoenix*, chapters 36 and 37.

162. *The Order of the Phoenix*, 739.

163. *The Order of the Phoenix*, 741.

164. *The Order of the Phoenix*, 740.

165. *The Philosopher's Stone*, 18.

166. *The Deathly Hallows*, 566.

167. *The Half-Blood Prince*, 603.

168. *The Deathly Hallows*, 295.

169. *The Philosopher's Stone*, 209.

170. *The Order of the Phoenix*, 469.

171. *The Order of the Phoenix*, 734.
172. *The Deathly Hallows*, 528.
173. *The Deathly Hallows*, 544.
174. *The Chamber of Secrets*, 31.
175. *The Goblet of Fire*, 620.
176. *The Half-Blood Prince*, 581.
177. *The Deathly Hallows*, 121.
178. *The Deathly Hallows*, 18.
179. *The Deathly Hallows*, 17–18.
180. *The Deathly Hallows*, 568.
181. *The Deathly Hallows*, 549.
182. *The Deathly Hallows*, 13.
183. *The Half-Blood Prince*, 415.
184. 1 John 4:16.
185. Augustine, *Confessions*, Book 10, chapter 27.
186. Matthew 25:14–30.
187. *The Half-Blood Prince*, 468.
188. *The Half-Blood Prince*, 523.
189. John Milton, *Paradise Lost*, Book 12, line 587.
190. *The Deathly Hallows*, 577.
191. *The Deathly Hallows*, 591.
192. *The Deathly Hallows*, 592.
193. *The Deathly Hallows*, 592–93.
194. *The Deathly Hallows*, 581.
195. *The Deathly Hallows*, 582.
196. *The Order of the Phoenix*, 719.
197. *The Half-Blood Prince*, 30–36.
198. *The Deathly Hallows*, 15.
199. *The Deathly Hallows*, 581.
200. *The Order of the Phoenix*, 716–17.
201. *The Deathly Hallows*, 16.
202. *The Deathly Hallows*, 581.
203. *The Half-Blood Prince*, 416.
204. John 15:15.

205. *The Half-Blood Prince*, 259–60.

206. *Coriolanus*, act 1, scene 3; Volumnia's second speech.

207. *The Half-Blood Prince*, 39.

208. *The Order of the Phoenix*, 710–11 and 714.

209. *The Deathly Hallows*, 589–90.

210. *The Order of the Phoenix*, 715.

211. *The Deathly Hallows*, 597.

212. *The Order of the Phoenix*, 743.

213. *The Philosopher's Stone*, 47.

214. *The Deathly Hallows*, 578.

215. 1 Corinthians 13:2.

7

It Is Essential That You Understand This

FREEDOM AND DETERMINATION

Dumbledore hazards a guess as to why Voldemort's parents, witch and Muggle, separate. His witch mother, Merope, has given his Muggle father, Tom Riddle (senior) a love potion. Dumbledore explains:

> "I believe that Merope, who was deeply in love with her husband, could not bear to continue enslaving him by magical means. I believe that she made the choice to stop giving him the potion."[1]

Merope, as is clear from Dumbledore's memories,[2] is not from a cultured and educated background, but she seems to understand a fundamental teaching in the Christian tradition: we can love only if we are free to give or not give that love. It follows that Merope's husband is not really loving her if he is behaving as he is because he is under the influence of a love potion. Even Amortentia, "the most powerful love potion in the world," Professor Slughorn explains, "doesn't

---

160

really create *love* of course."[3] Dumbledore's speculation implies that Merope is motivated by wanting to be really loved by her husband. In fact, when no longer under the influence of the potion, he simply leaves her.[4]

VOLDEMORT'S DETERMINISM

In contrast to Harry, Voldemort's truest nature is more like his father's than his mother's. He does not really love. Those he calls "friends" are, as Dumbledore observes, "more in the order of servants."[5] Voldemort never gives up the bullying behavior that characterizes him in the orphanage.[6] He is interested only in the manipulation of people by magic— the very manipulation that (if Dumbledore is right) his mother gave up in quest of love. In fact, not only does he not love, he does not even believe that people are free to love. He thinks that "there is only power and those too weak to seek it."[7] Underneath the struggle between Voldemort on the one hand, and Dumbledore, Harry, and others on the other hand, is a philosophical difference about human freedom.

This reaches its climax in the final confrontation between Harry and Voldemort. In it there are two opposed interpretations of the story. To Voldemort, Harry is "the boy who has survived by accident." Opposing this characterization of himself, Harry offers three deliberate choices that have been freely made. The first is his mother's: "Accident, was it, when my mother died to save me?" he asks. Her free choice of sacrifice is set against Voldemort's blind determinism. The next two deliberate choices are Harry's own. He faces Voldemort with these questions: "Accident, when I decided to fight in that graveyard? Accident, that I didn't defend myself tonight, and still survived, and returned to fight again?" Perhaps Voldemort feels threatened by this. He screams his reply: "*Accidents!*" The explanation he gives denies that Harry has made any difference by these choices.

As the watching crowd is frozen as if petrified, so that nobody seems to breathe but the two of them, Voldemort gives *his* account of what is behind Harry's story, an account that denies Harry the dignity of being a free agent having the courage to act: "Accident and chance, and the fact that you crouched and sniveled behind the skirts of greater men and women, and permitted me to kill them for you!" Harry's reply shows that his free choice of sacrifice made out of love has, in fact, made a difference: "You won't be killing anyone else tonight," he says. By that sacrifice, Harry has given people protection against Voldemort, protection that endures. He is able to tell his opponent, "You won't be able to kill any of them, ever again." Drawing attention to their different colored eyes, Harry's green and Voldemort's red, JK reinforces, as it were, what the facts of the plot say: that Harry's view is the one to go for, and Voldemort's is to be allowed to go no further. She is very clear.[8]

LEARNING ABOUT CHOICES

Harry does not always have such clarity about whether he can change what happens or whether it is simply something that is determined by the way things are. Like the lessons about love and sacrifice, this is something that he learns during his time at Hogwarts. He learns it first of all from his Headmaster. He brings to Dumbledore his anxiety about Tom Riddle's saying that there is likeness between them. He is troubled that this may indicate that he is fated to share in Riddle's evil. He confides to Dumbledore, "The Sorting Hat told me I'd—I'd have done well in Slytherin." When Dumbledore explains that Lord Voldemort, without meaning to, transferred some of his powers to Harry when he attacked him as a baby, Harry feels this means that he "*should* be in Slytherin." Dumbledore responds that the Sorting Hat placed Harry in Gryffindor, and invites him to think why that was. Harry, without realizing the importance of his answer, replies that it was because he asked not to go in Slytherin.

Dumbledore's interpretation of this reply sows the seed of the understanding that will enable Harry to successfully withstand Voldemort's claim that what has happened in his life is an accident. "*Exactly,*" Dumbledore tells Harry, "which makes you very *different* from Tom Riddle. It is our choices, Harry, that show what we truly are, far more than our abilities."[9] This last sentence is very important for understanding the teaching that Dumbledore gives Harry. He is saying it is not power that counts in the end, or (as Hermione has observed) cleverness.[10] What matters is what is chosen. The human person has freedom, and how that freedom is used matters more than what scope it may be given by a person's capabilities.

Dumbledore's teaching may be seen as a reprise of that of Moses, quoted at the beginning of the chapter on life and death: "See, I have set before you this day life and good, death and evil."[11] Our choices make for life and good, or death and evil. They end up making us who we are: virtue is the habit formed by repeated choices. Harry Potter's choices make him a person identified with life and good; Voldemort's make him a person identified with death and evil. Harry chooses to be who he is, but Dumbledore enables him to see his freedom of choice clearly. Not only is he encouraged to think it out: he is also given proof of the characterizing power of choices. Dumbledore shows Harry the Sword of Gryffindor, which he drew out of the Sorting Hat in the Chamber of Secrets, and says, "Only a true Gryffindor could have pulled that out of the hat, Harry."[12] Harry *chooses* to be in Gryffindor: he consequently becomes a true, brave Gryffindor.

In his third year, Harry needs encouragement from Dumbledore that his choice to spare Pettigrew's life does not render what he has done useless. Far from making no difference, Dumbledore points out, Harry has "helped uncover the truth" and "saved an innocent man from a terrible fate."[13] Harry is being taught that our decisions do make a difference: we are not simply blind victims of fate. He is also being taught that, further to his immediate accomplishments, the time may come when he will be very glad he saved Pettigrew's life.[14] It does indeed come, when Pettigrew hesitates to carry out Voldemort's command to kill him and a "tiny merciful impulse"[15] shows "magic at its deepest, its most impenetrable"[16]—the magic of the choice of clemency. Again in his sixth year, Dumbledore reminds Harry of the significance of choice. "Your mother had a choice,"[17] he says. The power of Lily Potter's sacrifice, of her love, comes from a deliberate choice to put her son's safety above her own survival.

CHOICES MAKING PEOPLE WHO THEY ARE

The truth that choice makes a difference is not only taught by Dumbledore: it is shown by what happens. Both Tom Riddle and Harry Potter are orphans. Both grow up in deprived circumstances. Tom grows up in an orphanage, "a grim place to grow up."[18] Harry grows up in Privet Drive. "Privet," as well as suggesting a type of hedge that corresponds to the Dursleys' conventionality, hints at "privation," and perhaps also a privacy that refuses community and fel-

lowship. Certainly, Harry is deprived. His early years boarding in Privet Drive are spent in a cupboard under the stairs,
with food not always provided.[19] He is often spoken of as
though he is not present. He is generally left out of outings.[20]
When not ignored, he is addressed as "Oi! You!"[21] For his
birthday, he does not get so much as a card from his family,[22]
and for Christmas he gets from them such presents as "a
toothpick,"[23] and "a single tissue."[24] These privations would
seem at least to equal those experienced by the young Tom,
in whose orphanage the orphans look "reasonably well-
cared-for."[25] Yet, Harry, by his choices, follows a very different path from Tom. Not only does he pass by the
opportunity to be helped on the way to greatness by being
in Slytherin House,[26] but he steadfastly refuses to be
seduced by the Dark Arts.[27] Tom, a Slytherin, achieves what
he thinks of as "greatness" by what he calls pushing "the
boundaries of magic further, perhaps, than they have ever
been pushed"[28]—that is, by the Dark Arts that the noble
would not use.[29]

Like Harry, Tom also becomes who he is by his choices,
which change not only his name[30] but even his appearance.
In the interview with Dumbledore when he is asking for a
job at Hogwarts, he already looks "less like Tom Riddle than
ever, his features thick with rage."[31] As a youngster he has a
"handsome face."[32] By his own choices, that face becomes
"whiter than a skull, with wide livid scarlet eyes, and a
nose...as flat as a snake's, with slits for nostrils."[33] He changes
so much that hardly anyone connects Lord Voldemort with
"the clever handsome boy who was once Head Boy" at
Hogwarts.[34]

Tom has become ugly by choice; he has become Lord
Voldemort by choice. In doing so, he chooses his own social
environment. When Dumbledore, who may be supposed to
be accurate in his perception, observes, "Lord Voldemort has

never had a friend, nor do I believe that he has ever wanted one,"[35] he is indicating that Voldemort's essential loneliness is chosen. In effect, Voldemort is choosing to commit to a lie, since it is not true that a person can flourish outside of human society. His project of greatness is therefore doomed. His manner of acting leads, in fact, to a diminution of his freedom, contrary to his view that his unrestrained use of magic (in effect, power) gives him a freedom to act that those whose use of magic is restrained (by love) do not have.[36]

VOLDEMORT'S
SELF-DEFEATING TYRANNY

Dumbledore explains to Harry how the tyrannical exercise of power constricts freedom by creating opposition:

> "If Voldemort had never murdered your father, would he have imparted in you a furious desire for revenge? Of course not! If he had not forced your mother to die for you, would he have given you a magical protection he could not penetrate? Of course not, Harry! Don't you see? Voldemort himself created his worst enemy, just as tyrants everywhere do! Have you any idea how much tyrants fear the people they oppress? All of them realize that, one day, amongst their many victims, there is sure to be one who rises against them and strikes back! Voldemort is no different!"[37]

Voldemort limits his freedom by turning Harry against him. Harry—and others who are fighting on the same side—destroy one by one the Horcruxes that Voldemort has made to increase his scope of action in the world, and it is in his conflict with Harry that Voldemort finally and definitively loses the life that enables him to act at all.[38]

Voldemort's lack of belief in freedom in the end limits his freedom to act. It has not, however, totally taken away his freedom to choose. He does choose his absolute friendlessness and absolute lovelessness. In effect, he chooses death and hell. To put this in terms of the Christian understanding of the Book of Genesis, he believes the serpent's lie that he "will be like God"[39] if he eats "of the tree of the knowledge of good and evil."[40] In other words, he believes that he will have the total freedom that belongs to God if he allows himself to act on the basis that what he wants (his desire) is right. He believes that pursuing his own desire for mastery as a final good will be effective in expanding his freedom to act. In fact, his lack of respect for the freedom of others limits his own freedom.

Freedom is freedom for all or it is not truly freedom. To put this in theological terms, freedom belongs to God, the source of every person's freedom, and it is only truly possessed in a positive relationship with God. In others words, it is by sharing the unbounded respect that God has for the freedom of every human person that we find our own true freedom. Or—to pursue Dumbledore's line of thought—tyrants always lose in the end, and respect for the other always wins.

The simplistic way the series works out these principles may seem to ignore the messy incompleteness of this world, a world in which the fullness of these principles being worked out is actually hidden in the final judgments of God. If this seems so, perhaps we need to remind ourselves that this is a children's story. It is not unreasonable for such a story to paint in broad strokes the template by which we would wish our children to assess their courses of action as they begin to take their place in the adult world.

Harry's True Freedom

Voldemort's negative modeling of values concerning freedom is contrasted with Harry's positive modeling of them. Voldemort tramples on the freedom of others and dies cut off from love—even the mischief-making poltergeist is delighted by his death.[41] Of Harry, who respects the freedom of others (that is, who loves), it is said, "They wanted him there with them." He is "an indispensable part" of what is going on.[42] Harry has become such by realizing his freedom, both in the sense of becoming aware of its reality and in the sense of translating that awareness into action. He learns about his freedom, as he learns about so much, from his Headmaster.

Harry and Dumbledore are discussing Trelawney's prediction, which says about Voldemort and Harry, "*Either must die at the hand of the other for neither can live while the other survives.*"[43] Dumbledore says, "You are setting too much store by the prophecy!"[44] In other words, Harry is thinking that what is to happen is more determined than it is, and that he has less freedom than he really does. The fourth time that Harry interrupts Dumbledore with "but," the latter, more agitated than Harry has ever seen him, says, "It is essential that you understand this!"[45] Dumbledore is a cool and relaxed person, so this agitation and these words point to the exceptional importance of Harry understanding his own freedom. It is so important because freedom is the necessary foundation of love.

Earlier in the conversation, when they are discussing the relative capabilities of Voldemort and Harry in the contest that is to unfold, Dumbledore says, "Harry, you can love."[46] As was indicated in the previous two chapters of this book, the ancient magic of sacrificial love weighs more heavily in the balance than the might of Voldemort's magic. To wield this magic, Harry must know that he is free. With this knowledge, he can choose to sacrifice his life and so protect both the magical community and the Muggles from Voldemort. That is why the Headmaster hammers the lesson of freedom into his pupil's head so urgently and so insistently. The fifth time Harry says "but," Dumbledore finally comes up with an argument that gets him to understand the lesson. He asks Harry to imagine that he had never heard of the prophecy, and asks Harry how he would feel about Voldemort. Harry realizes that he would "want him finished" and that he would want to do it himself. Dumbledore explains to Harry the conclusion that follows from this: "You see, the prophecy does not mean you *have* to do anything!" Harry is not being controlled by the prophecy—his behavior is not determined—he is making a free choice to confront Voldemort because of "all the terrible deeds" he has done.[47]

Voldemort, by contrast, has allowed himself to be controlled by the prophecy, in particular the part that says, "*The Dark Lord will mark him as his equal.*"[48] In doing this he has given Harry "the tools for the job" of finishing him off.[49] Voldemort, who believes that events are accidentally determined, has yielded up his own freedom to a prophecy, allowing his fate to be determined by it. Unlike Harry, he does not realize his freedom, either in the sense of becoming aware of its reality or in the sense of translating that awareness into action. Dumbledore explains this to his pupil, saying, "You are free to choose your way, quite free to turn your back on the prophecy! But Voldemort continues to set store by the prophecy."[50] Although Voldemort's action, which he allows to be determined, and Harry's action, which he freely chooses, lead them both to the same place and event—the final confrontation in the Great Hall[51]—there is, as Harry at last understands, "all the difference in the world" between their two paths.[52]

BAPTIZING Harry Potter

In a significant moment of intellectual growth and movement toward adulthood, Harry comes to share the awareness of personal freedom that characterizes his Headmaster and his parents. He knows that, as their paths converge, the difference between himself and Voldemort is "the difference between being dragged into the arena to face a battle to the death and walking into the arena with your head held high."[53] This difference is dramatically made plain in the final confrontation, in which Voldemort thinks he controls "the Wand of Destiny,"[54] but Harry is shown to be its "true master."[55] In the end, Voldemort, who neither believes in nor wins through to personal freedom, is controlled by a destiny to which he has foolishly submitted, and Harry, who both believes in and wins through to personal freedom, triumphs by his own choices.

These choices are reflections of the fundamental choice to take a stand against evil. Harry decides between "Horcruxes or Hallows,"[56] prioritizing the destruction of the power of evil to work in the world over his own personal power. He decides, for the sake of the same goal, on a "cold-blooded walk to his own destruction."[57] He decides to return to the fray from a place that is "warm and light and peaceful"[58] for the sake of ensuring that "fewer souls are maimed, fewer families are torn apart."[59] Before this final confrontation with Voldemort, Dumbledore underlines Harry's freedom one last time, telling him it is up to him whether he goes back. "I've got a choice?" Harry asks, and Dumbledore answers, "Oh yes."[60] His final choice, after Voldemort's death, is to put the Elder Wand back where it came from.[61] For this, he needs no reassurance from his teacher that he has a choice. He is truly free.

All that remains is for him to pass on the teaching about freedom to the next generation. He tells his son Albus Severus, "The Sorting Hat takes your choice into account....

170

It did for me"[62]—meaning that the Sorting Hat interrogates not only ability but also will. Harry's son receives with wonder this teaching about personal freedom (learned by experience as well as by instruction). As he begins at Hogwarts, he will know that it is not "luck and chance" (as Voldemort would have it)[63] that determine outcomes but the free exercise of choice. The Sorting Hat is a kind of distant intimation of the final division to be made, not into the four houses of Hogwarts, but—according to the parable in Saint Matthew's Gospel—into sheep and goats, into eternal life and eternal punishment.[64] And there is another spiritual message that it has to communicate. This is the subject of the next chapter.

Notes

1. *The Half-Blood Prince*, 203.
2. *The Half-Blood Prince*, chapter 10.
3. *The Half-Blood Prince*, 176–77.
4. *The Half-Blood Prince*, 203.
5. *The Half-Blood Prince*, 416.
6. *The Half-Blood Prince*, 250.
7. *The Philosopher's Stone*, 211.
8. *The Deathly Hallows*, 591.
9. *The Chamber of Secrets*, 244–45.
10. *The Philosopher's Stone*, 208.
11. Deuteronomy 30:15 (Revised Standard Version).
12. *The Chamber of Secrets*, 245.
13. *The Prisoner of Azkaban*, 310.
14. *The Prisoner of Azkaban*, 311.
15. *The Deathly Hallows*, 381.
16. *The Prisoner of Azkaban*, 311.
17. *The Half-Blood Prince*, 246.
18. *The Half-Blood Prince*, 251.
19. *The Philosopher's Stone*, 26.

20. *The Philosopher's Stone*, 22.
21. *The Deathly Hallows*, 31.
22. *The Prisoner of Azkaban*, 12.
23. *The Chamber of Secrets*, 158.
24. *The Goblet of Fire*, 357.
25. *The Half-Blood Prince*, 251.
26. *The Philosopher's Stone*, 91.
27. *The Half-Blood Prince*, 477.
28. *The Half-Blood Prince*, 415.
29. *The Philosopher's Stone*, 14.
30. *The Chamber of Secrets*, 231.
31. *The Half-Blood Prince*, 417.
32. *The Half-Blood Prince*, 346.
33. *The Goblet of Fire*, 558.
34. *The Chamber of Secrets*, 242.
35. *The Half-Blood Prince*, 260.
36. *The Half-Blood Prince*, 415.
37. *The Half-Blood Prince*, 476–77.
38. *The Deathly Hallows*, 596.
39. Genesis 3:5.
40. Genesis 2:17.
41. *The Deathly Hallows*, 597.
42. *The Deathly Hallows*, 596.
43. *The Order of the Phoenix*, 741.
44. *The Half-Blood Prince*, 476.
45. *The Half-Blood Prince*, 477.
46. *The Half-Blood Prince*, 476.
47. *The Half-Blood Prince*, 478.
48. *The Order of the Phoenix*, 741.
49. *The Half-Blood Prince*, 477.
50. *The Half-Blood Prince*, 479.
51. *The Deathly Hallows*, chapter 36.
52. *The Half-Blood Prince*, 479.
53. *The Half-Blood Prince*, 479.

54. *The Deathly Hallows*, 594.
55. *The Deathly Hallows*, 595.
56. *The Deathly Hallows*, 392.
57. *The Deathly Hallows*, 555.
58. *The Deathly Hallows*, 579.
59. *The Deathly Hallows*, 578.
60. *The Deathly Hallows*, 578.
61. *The Deathly Hallows*, 600.
62. *The Deathly Hallows*, 607.
63. *The Deathly Hallows*, 13.
64. Matthew 25:31–46.

8

A Pretty Boring Life

THE HIDDEN AND THE OSTENTATIOUS

"It's got to be a pretty boring life, hasn't it, being a hat?" says Ron.[1] And indeed, the hat in question does not have the accoutrements of glamour: it is "an extremely old, dirty, patched wizard's hat."[2] In appearance it seems to invite the dismissal that goes with the phrase (contained within its description) *old hat*. Certainly that is Voldemort's view. When the "patched, frayed, and dirty" Sorting Hat is dropped at Harry's feet by Dumbledore's magical bird, Voldemort laughs.[3] "An old hat," he mocks, and asks, "Do you feel brave, Harry Potter? Do you feel safe now?"[4] Yet the hat delivers the Sword of Gryffindor by which the Basilisk is defeated.[5] It saves Harry and Ginny. It makes possible, therefore, the birth of their children.

Old hat is a description often given to traditional teaching, which, like Fawkes's delivery to Harry, can seem simply a "ragged thing."[6] Yet this teaching, for all Voldemort's mockery, enables his defeat, as the examination of some of its themes in the preceding chapters has shown. The old hat symbolizes a further aspect of traditional teaching: its hiddenness and its relinquishment of outward display. The hat's first words are:

> *"Oh, you may not think I am pretty,*
> *But don't judge on what you see"*

It immediately goes on to sing:

> *"I'll eat myself if you can find*
> *A smarter hat than me."*[7]

Its wisdom is, ultimately, the wisdom of love. It respects the individuality of the pupils, paying careful attention to their abilities and ambitions, yet at the same time it is aware of the need for unity as it sings (branching out a bit) in Harry's fifth year:

> *"Our Hogwarts is in danger*
> *From external, deadly foes*
> *And we must unite inside her*
> *Or we'll crumble from within."*[8]

Hidden Virtue

This wisdom of love is cloaked by the hat's outward lack of prettiness. The hat's lack of prettiness also conceals its ability to deliver powerful help to those in need. From it comes the Sword of Gryffindor, symbol and agent of courage, both in the Chamber of Secrets[9] and outside the castle after Voldemort forces the hat on Neville's head.[10] Voldemort's contempt for the "patched, frayed, and dirty"[11] hat in both these episodes recalls the contest in Shakespeare's play *The Merchant of Venice*, in which suitors of Portia have to choose from among gold, silver, and lead caskets. The one choosing the casket that contains her portrait wins her hand in marriage. It is in the lead casket, and the one who chooses it does so "not by the view."[12] He rejects the gold and silver caskets because he associates those metals with the concealment of evil with outward show. It is the lack of show that attracts him to the lead.

This story echoes the basic Christian theme of virtue being hidden in what is outwardly unattractive. It draws its inspiration from the One of whom the prophet Isaiah wrote, "He had no form or majesty that we should look at him, nothing in his appearance that we should desire him." Like the lead casket in the eyes of the failing suitors, he is "despised" and held "of no account."[13] The Sorting Hat shares in this apparent worthlessness and yet is a source of wisdom, love, and courage. Voldemort, who despises the hat, is like the suitors that despise the lead casket. He is a loser. "There will be no more Sorting at Hogwarts School," he announces, thinking that "the emblem, shield, and colors" of his ancestor Salazar Slytherin will suffice for all.[14] His contempt for the hat reflects his contempt for difference, for otherness: in short, for all that is not himself. It is precisely that which makes him a loser. His wanting to impose his own identity on others, as well as his refusal to allow others to have any colors but his own, in the end makes others the enemies who will destroy him. The Sorting Hat looks "empty and ragged"[15] in his hand, but he is the one who is empty. His life is in what is exterior, in his (necessarily unstable) control of others, and so is doomed. He has no inner life. Yet the hat is less empty than it seems. Neville draws the Sword of Gryffindor "from its depths."[16] The hat, the outwardly "mildewed object,"[17] conceals the object that represents strength and courage. Through these magical objects, the story is saying that true strength and courage can be hidden within a life that outwardly fails to make an impression.

This is also shown in the life of Neville Longbottom. *Longbottom* rather implies that he has hidden depths, and so it proves. On his first appearance in the story, he is telling his grandmother that he has lost his toad, not the coolest of creatures.[18] He is so forgetful that his grandmother sends him a Remembrall to remind him when he has forgotten something.[19] He is noticeably lacking in confidence, being rather under his grandmother's sway,[20] and, as Luna Lovegood observes with "embarrassing honesty," is (like her) not as cool as might be expected for a friend of Harry Potter.[21] However, Neville's courageous taking of a stand against his friends at the end of his first year intimates that he has hidden depths of courage,[22] and this is abundantly clear in his slaying of Nagini in the final confrontation with Voldemort.[23] Furthermore, he is, as far as we know, the only pupil in the story who goes on to become a professor at Hogwarts.[24] True strength and courage are indeed hidden within Neville's life, which outwardly fails to make an impression.

Freedom from the need to make an impression—in other words, freedom from enslavement to what is external—is connected with this strength and courage. An heir to the valor of Gryffindor cannot live needing to cut a fine figure. He or she needs to be brave enough to accept obscurity, misunderstanding, and even contempt. This corresponds to traditional Christian wisdom. The *Imitation of Christ* urges its reader to take delight in being unknown and unregarded.[25] In hiddenness, true virtue grows. Free from the distortions of flattery, an inner goodness grows. Dumbledore's whole game plan for Harry rests on this truth. He arranges for Harry to have, like the hat, a pretty boring life. Professor McGonagall protests that the Dursleys, with whom

Dumbledore is placing Harry, "will never understand him! He'll be famous!" Dumbledore responds,

> "It would be enough to turn any boy's head. Famous before he can walk and talk! Famous for something he won't even remember! Can't you see how much better off he'll be, growing up away from all that until he's ready to take it?"[26]

This corresponds to traditional Christian wisdom about the value of the hidden (even cloistered) life.

THE OBSCURE AND THE ORDINARY

Sometimes this hidden life is linked to the time that Jesus spent at Nazareth, hidden from the world. It is absurd, of course, to suggest that Mr. and Mrs. Dursley have the parenting skills of Mary and Joseph. The parallel is in the obscurity. Just as every child in the magical world already knows Harry's name,[27] so every child of Israel knows about the Messiah, and yet they are both hidden. The cupboard under the stairs is not the manger, yet at least one Christian saint (Louis de Montfort) is reputed to have lived in such a place. Obscurity ensures that there is nothing to turn Harry's head, nothing to make him proud.[28] He develops a true heart instead of a giant, fame-fed ego. The hard time he gets from the Dursleys helps this, insofar as it saves him from "the appalling damage" (Dumbledore's words) inflicted on the "unfortunate" Dudley by dint of over-indulgence.[29] Dumbledore is able to tell Harry (at the end of his fifth year),

> "You arrived at Hogwarts, neither as happy nor as well-nourished as I would have liked, perhaps, yet alive and healthy. You were not a pampered little

prince, but as normal a boy as I could have hoped under the circumstances."[30]

Dumbledore's plan works well in giving Harry protection from the external danger of Voldemort. The plan also gives him an ordinary life. This ordinary life is a protection from the spiritual danger of pride, while being an aid to humility.

Voldemort does not escape this danger. He has contempt for anything that makes him ordinary, such as his name Tom. He wants to be "different, separate, notorious."[31] Harry, on the other hand, never tries to avoid his name, although the Dursleys think it a "nasty common name."[32] He interiorizes the value of being ordinary. At Hogwarts, detentions are sometimes given which involve doing things without magic.[33] This is not welcome to those being punished, but it has the advantage of keeping them from the self-complacency of the flick of the wand. By the end of his education at Hogwarts, Harry is spiritually wise enough to be able to choose this option for himself. For example, he digs Dobby's grave without magic, finding himself "relishing the manual work, glorying in the non-magic of it."[34] This recalls the monastic practice of manual labor as a spiritual discipline.

It is not being argued that using magic is equivalent to being proud. The Weasley household shows that magic can find a context where it is perfectly normal. Rather, the argument is that magic can be used in the service of pride, so that it is a means of drawing attention to oneself as extraordinary. This is what the monastic tradition calls singularity, the vice that is the opposite of the virtue of accepting one's ordinariness. Voldemort certainly uses magic in this way, as do, more innocently, the magicians who gather for the World Cup at the Muggle camping site, causing Mr. Weasley to observe, "We can't resist showing off when we get together."[35]

HARRY MOCKED AND MISUNDERSTOOD

Harry's isolation at 4 Privet Drive ensures that he is kept from the temptation of showing off. There, even the use of the word *magic* is enough to provoke a thunderous reaction.[36] He is not famous there.[37] Until he becomes old enough to go to Hogwarts, he is as unaware that he is special and famous as he was when he was left asleep on the doorstep of 4 Privet Drive.[38] When this awareness does come, it comes in a form that isn't likely to turn his head. He is mocked for being well known. Publicity becomes a bitter draught for him to drink. An early sample of this comes in his first Potions lessons, when Professor Snape announces him, to snickers, as "our new—*celebrity*."[39] As he goes to buy his books for his second year at Hogwarts, he is dragged to the fore by the publicity-addicted Gilderoy Lockhart, to be photographed for the front page of the *Daily Prophet*.[40] He is mocked for being famous, despite—as Ginny points out—his not wanting what happened.[41] The attention he gets turns very unpleasant when, later in the school year, his ability to speak Parseltongue marks him out as a possible descendant of Salazar Slytherin,[42] and he is suspected of being guilty of a petrifying attack.[43] In fact, far from being Slytherin's descendant, he is the last descendant of Ignotus Peverell.[44]

Ignotus means "unknown" in Latin, and this is what truly characterizes Harry. He is hidden (under the stairs)[45] at the start of the story, and he hides himself (under his Invisibility Cloak) at the end of the story, as he goes to his confrontation with Voldemort, both in the forest[46] and in the Great Hall.[47] Harry is unknown, and that is the source of both his greatness (because he is not a slave to ego-flattering fame) and his suffering (because he is misunderstood and maligned). This suffering is intensified in his fourth year at Hogwarts, when his name comes out of the Goblet of Fire;[48] even his best friend, Ron, doesn't believe he didn't put it there himself in quest of glory.[49] Although Ron in time comes to believe him,[50] Harry has to face an even greater burden of obloquy in his next year, when half the people at Hogwarts think him "strange, even mad," following the lead of the *Daily Prophet*.[51] This paper writes about him as though he is a "deluded, attention-seeking person who thinks he's a great tragic hero or something." The defamation is in order to discredit his word, since this communicates the unpalatable truth that Voldemort has returned. Harry is presented as someone who "loves being famous," which is a very bitter lie for him to hear, as his fame is linked to the murder of his parents.[52] The negative publicity about Harry reaches its apogee in his final year of school, when he is known simply as "Undesirable No. 1."[53]

All of this calumny has the same sort of effect on Harry as Dumbledore's placing him with the Dursleys. It stops his head from being turned by his fame. In fact, it goes further than this. It gives him a spiritual purity in the sense that it scours away any love of outward show, any wish to live by the impression he makes on others. It gives him a lonely independence, so that he is able to act from his own depth. As he goes to fulfill "his true destiny,"[54] which as far as he knows is his death, he is able to walk, hidden from view, past the woman he loves, without speaking, without looking back.[55] This ability to act alone contrasts him with Voldemort, who needs others. That need is apparent in Voldemort's possession of Quirrell.[56]

The Shallowness of Voldemort and Lockhart

Voldemort's shallowness is apparent in the way Pettigrew has to do his work for him[57] and then has to carry him to his rebirthing.[58] Above all, it is apparent in his need to be encircled by Death Eaters.[59] Yet Voldemort is not truly in relationship with any of these people. He is connected to them only by magic, manipulation, and threats. To be truly in relation with others, he would need, like Harry, to be capable of acting from within his own depth. He would need to be able to act *without* them. Voldemort, who wants to be independent, cannot truly act alone. Harry, who has learned to be his own man, can, which is why in the end he is surrounded by people "trying to hug some part of him, hundreds of them pressing in."[60] It is also why he is able to be truly in relation to others. Voldemort lives outwardly, in his domination of others; Harry lives inwardly, in the purity of his own being.

Voldemort's life is a tragic contrast to Harry's. Lockhart's is a comic contrast. Yet he too lives outwardly. He works to get publicity by taking credit for what other people have done, and manipulates them, not just by his charming smile,[61] but by Memory Charms.[62] His sinister heart is revealed when he tries to destroy the minds of Harry and Ron.[63] The ludicrous vanity of his posturing is clear in his stated ambition "to rid the world of evil and market…[his] own range of hair-care potions."[64] Lockhart's ostentation contrasts with Harry's hiddenness. His true self comes out, just as Harry's does, when he is faced with danger. When the "five times winner of *Witch Weekly's* Most-Charming-Smile Award"[65] is asked by his colleagues to make good his boast that he can tackle the monster in the Chamber of Secrets, he no longer looks remotely handsome. His lip trembles, and, in the absence of his usually toothy grin, he looks weak-chinned and weedy.[66] His lack of inner depth and courage makes clear by contrast Harry's own growth in these qualities during his Hogwarts years. Harry, for example, realizes that he has left "not only the ground behind, but also his fear," as he looks down on the Hungarian Horntail dragon from his Firebolt.[67] Danger brings out his true courage.

RON IN THE SHADOWS

The spiritual value of being hidden, as well as the suffering that it involves, is explored, not just in Harry and the obvious contrast to Voldemort and Lockhart, but also in other characters who exemplify it. In Ron's case, the suffering is to the fore, although as he grows he gains mastery over his natural antipathy to being in Harry's shadow, a spiritually significant development. Hermione explains Ron's struggle with obscurity after he and Harry have fallen out because Ron doesn't believe that Harry didn't enter himself for the Triwizard Tournament. She tells Harry that Ron is jealous, and that:

> "Ron's got all those brothers to compete against at home, and you're his best friend, and you're really famous—he's always shunted to one side whenever people see you, and he puts up with it, and he never mentions it, but I suppose this is just one time too many."[68]

It is Ron's concern for Harry that overcomes his distance from him. When he sees the real danger that Harry is in during the first task, he changes his mind about whether Harry has put his own name in the Goblet of Fire.[69] Ron's love for Harry as a friend is stronger than the suspicion born of—or at least encouraged by—his being overshadowed by him. Ron grows and their friendship deepens through this crisis. It is not the final one, however. In the last book, there is a crisis in which the issue is not simply Harry being more popular than Ron with people in general: the crisis is about whether he is more popular with the woman that Ron loves.

In traditional Christian spiritual writing, it is the devil who tempts people according to their particular weaknesses and vulnerabilities. Ron's struggle with the locket Horcrux echoes the struggles of monks with the temptations of the devil, right back to Antony of the Desert. Indeed, it goes even further back: it echoes the temptations of Jesus.[70] Riddle speaks to Ron as the devil speaks to Jesus in the desert. The material of the temptation is similar: in both cases it touches on cutting a figure. Jesus is tempted to throw himself off the pinnacle of the Temple so as to be miraculously saved and become the focus of attention;[71] Ron is tempted to despair because he is not the focus of attention. Out of the Horcrux, the voice hisses: *"Least loved, always, by the mother who craved a daughter...least loved, now, by the girl who prefers your friend...second best, always, eternally overshadowed..."*[72] His tempter plays on his suspicion that both his mother and Hermione prefer Harry to himself. Ron is filled with anguish, but he destroys the Horcrux with Gryffindor's courage and sword, and sinks to his knees, weeping.[73] He has won the battle with the tempter. Friendship has overcome fear of being overshadowed.

The issue of Harry being more famous than Ron does come up again, but this time it is a joke. Ron is able to laugh at it. A great number of faces seem to be turned toward Harry, as he sees his children onto the Hogwarts Express, and when his son Albus asks why they are all staring, Ron says, with the self-mockery of one who has got over the whole issue, "It's me. I'm extremely famous."[74] He is spiritually mature. He has learned to live in obscurity.

SECRETS OF SIRIUS AND SNAPE

Ron is not the only one who faces obscurity. Sirius Black is in a more difficult position with regard to being truly known than either Ron or Harry. When Harry is abreacting from the shock of reading Percy's letter advising Ron to sever ties with him, he reflects:

> Nearly everyone in the wizarding world thought Sirius a dangerous murderer and a great Voldemort supporter and he had had to live with that knowledge for fourteen years.[75]

Even when he is being very generous, Sirius has to act anonymously, following the gospel injunction, "Do not let your left hand know what your right hand is doing."[76] This is the case with his Christmas gift to his godson,[77] which remains anonymous until he is able, much later, to write to Harry, "It was I who sent you the Firebolt."[78] Harry himself follows in the footsteps of his godfather the year after he receives his Firebolt, when he gives a gift that—mainly because of Mrs. Weasley—has to remain largely hidden: the gift of his Triwizard Tournament winnings to Fred and George, so that they can start their joke shop.[79]

The gospel explains the spiritual value of giving without being known as the giver, saying: "Your Father who sees in secret will reward you."[80] In other words, the gift will be known by God, who will bless the giver. It can be said that such giving is done simply because it is good: for the sake of goodness itself. If giving is known by others, it remains possible that it will be done for the sake of the impression it makes on others, whether recipients or observers. Only by being anonymous can a giver avoid these dangers and grow in real goodness. This is why, of course, many gifts are made anonymously.

The Harry Potter story shows us people in situations where they have no choice but to act anonymously in such things as giving. It shows us people whose circumstances have helped them to grow in real goodness. The difficulties that appear simply burdens are disguised blessings, forging stronger souls. They can help people find the path of hiddenness. Self-effacement, acting in a hidden way, is a Christian value, which is reflected in JK's narrative. Against all expectation (on a first reading), the character who embodies this value to the highest degree is Severus Snape.

It is only after his death that the full extent of Snape's heroism becomes apparent. Entering the memories that Snape gives in his dying moments, Harry is witness in the Pensieve to an interview between Dumbledore and Snape that is the final resolution of the ongoing debate among him, Ron, and Hermione about Snape's true intentions. Dumbledore says to Snape, "Help me protect Lily's son."[81] He finally consents, with a condition that has huge implications:

> "Very well. Very well. But never—never tell, Dumbledore! This must be between us! Swear it! I cannot bear...especially Potter's son...I want your word!"
>
> "My word, Severus, that I shall never reveal the best of you?" Dumbledore sighed, looking down into Snape's ferocious, anguished face. "If you insist..."[82]

If Snape's motive for secrecy is not wanting to be seen doing anything for the son of the one who has humiliated him,[83] his motive for agreeing to do what Dumbledore asks is love for that son's mother. Since her death means that he cannot now win her love, and since he is hardly likely to get thanks from Harry who inherits the antipathetic relationship that his father had with Snape, it is an extraordinarily pure love. It is also hidden.

So too is his heroism in the fight against Voldemort. This is hidden under the appearance of its opposite. Snape has to appear to be indifferent to a colleague (Charity Burbage), who begs for his help before she is callously murdered.[84] He endures an even greater chasm between what people think of as his motivation and what it really is when he kills Dumbledore at the latter's request.[85] With Dumbledore dead, there is no one at all left who understands that Snape is, in fact, working against Voldemort. This is only possible because of Snape's skill as an Occlumens.[86] His Occlumency is the ultimate hiding of the good he does. It is, as it were, at the opposite end of the spectrum from the Memory Charms that Lockhart uses to create a fiction of heroism.[87] Snape is a hero who hides the fact; Lockhart is a coward who pretends to be a hero and advertises his pretension. Snape's "unfathomable"[88] expression hides the real wellsprings of his being. It hides his undying devotion to Lily Potter. It hides the real motivation for all he does—love.

The spiritual value of hiding the goodness of one's heart—Snape's heart is good, if damaged and flawed—is that one does not get caught up in the unreality that other people's adulation can foster. It is a way of avoiding the idolizing of self. Also important to this is an awareness of one's own weakness and emptiness: it is not enough to avoid other people's adulation if one supplies one's own. This means knowing the reality of one's brokenness. Because of his particular history, this is not a difficulty for Snape. He is not likely to forget his worst memory.[89] He is not likely to forget that he was called "Snivellus."[90] And he is humbled in the depths of his soul by the memory that he once called the love of his life a Mudblood.[91]

The "unforgivable word"[92] that leads to the parting of the ways between him and Lily means that his soul resonates unfalteringly with the words of the penitential psalm, "My sin is ever before me."[93] It means that Snape is safe from pride, first enemy of the soul. He can live a life destined for beatitude, a life that evokes the promise of the first beatitude, which sums up all of the Sermon on the Mount: "Blessed are the poor in spirit, for theirs is the kingdom of heaven."[94] Snape knows his spiritual poverty. Slumped before Dumbledore, "a hundred years of misery" in his face,[95] he knows he has nothing, and in his nothingness he binds himself to give protection to Harry.[96] This gift is hidden almost even from his own heart, since the love for Harry's mother that motivates the gift is all but occluded by the painful aversion for his tormentor, Harry's father. Snape's gift remains pure, because the commitment is not revealed till after the giver's death.

THE HUMILITY OF RON AND HARRY

The spiritual principle of humility, of not allowing oneself to be dazzled by the supposed goodness of one's actions, is also illustrated in the lives of Ron and Harry. When Ron returns after abandoning Harry and Hermione, he is not proud of saving Harry's life and destroying the locket Horcrux. He says "I'm sorry I left. I know I was a—a—" and looks around at the darkness, "as if hoping a bad enough word would swoop down upon him and claim him."[97] Ron, like Snape, is aware of his failure, and so his good deeds are grounded in the humility that alone can protect his soul from pride. He, like Snape, has the attitude, "My sin is ever before me."[98] Ron knows the reality of his own poverty of spirit. He knows his own brokenness and weakness. He knows that inwardly he is not cool. The stardust of the seemingly heroic is not going to blind his spiritual sight. In his poverty of spirit, he receives a pledge of that final blessedness that belongs to heaven: a fraternal hug from Harry.[99] Harry receives this hug in poverty of spirit also.

He too knows that inwardly he is not cool. His words of two years before show this. With a heart that is humble, if not free from the flaw of intemperate anger, he tells Ron and Hermione the reality of his encounters with Voldemort:

> "I didn't get through any of that because I was brilliant at Defence Against the Dark Arts, I got through it all because—because help came at the right time, or because I guessed right—but I just blundered through it all, I didn't have a clue what I was doing—"[100]

This is part of what Harry seems to have in mind when he tells Ron that he has been trying to tell him for years that heroic stuff always sounds cooler than it really was.[101] He may also be recalling what he said in the Hog's Head, concerning his exploits: "I had a lot of help with all that stuff."[102] Harry knows from experience that the way this sort of thing is imagined is very different from the reality. The night that Dumbledore announces the Triwizard Tournament, Harry lies in bed and in his mind he is "standing in the grounds, his arms raised in triumph in front of the whole school," with everyone applauding and screaming.[103] He does win the Tournament, but it is "a nightmare."[104] He is protected both from other people's fantasies about his heroism and from his own. His soul is hidden from danger.

Saint Paul writes to the Colossians, "You have died, and your life is hidden with Christ in God."[105] If we take *died* to refer to the death of egotistical fantasies of heroism (baptism into the Christian faith carries this implication), and take *Christ* to refer to participation in his suffering (Harry is hit with the *Crucio* Curse—the Latin word means "I crucify"[106]), then Saint Paul's epistle could be written to Harry when he comes back from confronting Lord Voldemort in the graveyard. Hiddenness is of the essence of spiritual life.

THE INVISIBILITY CLOAK

This chapter began with a consideration of the Sorting Hat, a magical object whose glory is hidden by its appearance. There is, of course, another magical object that plays a large part in the series that is very explicitly linked to the spiritual value of hiddenness: the Invisibility Cloak. In "The Tale of the Three Brothers," choosing the cloak is linked to humility and wisdom:

> *The youngest brother was the humblest and also the wisest of the brothers, and he did not trust Death. So he asked for something that would enable him to go forth from that place without being followed by Death. And Death, most unwillingly, handed over his own Cloak of Invisibility.*

This choice is contrasted to the ones made by those who are not humble or wise. The second brother is "an arrogant man," who asks for "the power to recall others from Death." The first brother is "a combative man," who asks for "a wand more powerful than any in existence." Both these other choices are about gaining power, and what was said about power and weakness applies to them. Like Voldemort, the brothers find that the pursuit of power leads them to weakness and death. The second brother is drawn to the dead among whom he seeks his love. The first brother attracts attention to himself by boasting of his powerful wand, and he gets murdered following its theft.[107] This is a pattern that is repeated, according to the legend surrounding this wand. As Hermione says, it would be "bound to attract trouble." One of its names is "the Deathstick," and this can be taken to refer not just to the death that it deals out, but also the death that it brings to its owner, who tends to get murdered by others in quest of the power that the wand brings.[108]

Unlike his brothers, the youngest of the three is not found by Death.[109] On the simplest level of interpretation, he is not found because he is invisible. On a spiritual level of interpretation, the youngest brother's hiddenness denotes humility. This means that he avoids pride, which is a source of death—both practically speaking, as pride tends to antagonize other people, and theologically speaking, since pride separates one from God, who is the source of life. The practical and the theological are linked, since God is love[110]—honoring God entails showing humble love to others. The humility that avoids death by not antagonizing people also avoids "the second death,"[111] or damnation, by not refusing to accept God. It could also be said to avoid the snares of the devil, who needs human weakness—above all, pride—to help him in his work. Being hidden, in the sense of being humble, means being invisible to the devil. Like the Invisibility Cloak that symbolizes it, this humble hiddenness "endures eternally, giving constant and impenetrable concealment, no matter what spells are cast at it."[112] This humble hiddenness brings one to eternal life. As the Bible says, "Those who humble themselves will be exalted."[113]

It is perhaps no accident that magic (as described by JK) itself is normally hidden. The signing of the International Statute of Secrecy marks the year (1689) when wizards go into hiding for good.[114] It is significant that Voldemort wants to repeal this statute.[115] In his "Magic is might" way of thinking, Muggles should know that wizards and witches are their true rulers. They are to be terrorized into submission. In Dumbledore's way of thinking, magic should rather be associated with love, and it is characteristic of love to want to get out of the way, not to impose itself on others. Love (as Saint Paul says) "is not envious or boastful or arrogant or rude. It does not insist on its own way; it is not irritable or resentful."[116] When a person loves, his or her ego wears an Invisibility Cloak. Dumbledore, whose calm, courteous, and restrained personality governs Hogwarts, is a great Headmaster, and the school cannot be found by any Muggle. All Muggles see when they reach Hogwarts is "a mouldering old ruin with a sign over the entrance saying DANGER, DO NOT ENTER, UNSAFE."[117] This is a kind of loving courtesy: Muggles are not going to be imposed upon by any ostentatious or alarming display of magic. Hogwarts presents a humble aspect to them.

It is its Headmaster, Dumbledore, who gives Harry his Invisibility Cloak, with a note saying, "Use it well."[118] As his teacher, Dumbledore would want Harry to learn true invisibility, invisibility of the ego, in order to escape the devil and death, in both the physical and the spiritual sense. The cloak comes from Harry's father,[119] but the latter inherited it. Its first owner, Ignotus Peverell, is buried at Godric's Hollow,[120] Harry's first home.[121] "The Tale of the Three Brothers," woven around Ignotus and his brothers,[122] has a special aptness to Harry. The youngest brother eventually, "at a great age," takes off his Cloak of Invisibility and gives it to his son. The story continues:

> And then he greeted Death as an old friend, and went with him gladly, and, equals, they departed this life.[123]

The clear implication of this last sentence of the story is that the youngest brother dies serenely, and at the same time Death leaves this life. In other words, when Ignotus dies, Death is conquered. This is true in the sense of the youngest brother having mastered Death by his long life and by his serene acceptance of dying, but also in the sense that Death departing this life indicates that somehow the world is rid of death. All this corresponds to what happens to Harry. Thanks to the Invisibility Cloak, whose perfect impenetrability thwarts the hope of "some tiny part of him...to be sensed, to be seen, to be stopped,"[124] he is able to triumph over his lesser nature, which might let him be persuaded to abandon his mission. He goes, accepting that he will die. His encounter with Voldemort leads to Death departing this life in that Voldemort and his Death Eaters no longer carry out arbitrary killings. This arbitrary death dealing is defeated by Harry going, as he supposes, to his own death.

Harry's going to his death is, as we have seen, linked to Christ's going to his death. The Invisibility Cloak hides him, and this hiddenness is linked to humility, the humility that characterized Christ. It is apt that the cloak is a Hallow, for the word *hallow* means "holy." The cloak's magic is connected not only with the humility that characterizes holiness, but also with the altruism that is essential to it. Dumbledore explains to Harry that "its true magic...is that it can be used to protect and shield others as well as its owner."[125] The cloak is the only Hallow that Harry keeps. He leaves the Resurrection Stone in the forest. Dumbledore calls this "a wise and courageous decision."[126] He watches Harry "with enormous affection and admiration" as he announces his intention to foreswear the use of the Elder Wand.[127] (His own wand, which he uses instead, has holly in it, traditionally associated with holiness, and a phoenix feather, token of the resurrection.)[128] Dumbledore beams at Harry's decision to keep the cloak, saying, "It is yours forever, until you pass it on!"[129] The implication is that Harry is right to single out the cloak as the only one he keeps.

As in the tale, the brother who chose the cloak was the only one to outsmart Death; so, in his own story, Harry is making the choice of life by opting for the cloak. The Elder Wand would have led to antagonistic and maybe fatal relations with others; the Resurrection Stone would have involved him in unhealthy longings for the realm of Death. The cloak alone hides him from pride and conflict; it alone gives him the cover he needs from material and spiritual threats to lead his life to the full. In choosing the cloak, Harry is choosing the former of the two choices that Moses puts before his people when he says, "See, I have set before you this day life and good, death and evil."[130] Dumbledore's evident approval of Harry as he makes his choice of the cloak is the approval of a Headmaster who has seen his pupil learn, not just the technique that his school teaches (such as the *Expelliarmus* spell), but also its spiritual values. In the end, Harry stands before Dumbledore's portrait, and "the pride and gratitude emanating from him"[131] is the Headmaster's reaction to Harry's spiritual maturity. Harry has become a person committed to life.

This is final culmination of a learning process that begins with the painful hiddenness with the Dursleys that teaches Harry humility. At number 4 Privet Drive, Harry is invisible in the sense that no one pays any attention to what he wants. At Hogwarts, the cloak accompanies Harry in his adventures and makes possible his learning of spiritual lessons. It is thanks to the cloak that, in his first year, he is able to reach a place where he can see his heart's desire.[132] Hidden from others, he is alone with his heart, like a monk praying in the night. Harry soon extends the use of the cloak to Ron and Hermione,[133] and together they confront Voldemort.[134]

Humility and fellowship are the fundamental values associated with the cloak, but Harry does not reach full maturity in using the cloak all at once. He uses it to enable him to throw mud at Malfoy,[135] but also to help him and his friends show solidarity with Hagrid at the time of his need.[136] He uses it in his misguided attempt to go, as he thinks, to Sirius's rescue;[137] to hide in Tottenham Court Road, where he is under threat from Death Eaters;[138] and to go with Hermione to Godric's Hollow,[139] where they almost fall foul of Voldemort.[140] These uses of the cloak are, as it were, Harry's practice—some good, some less so—in using the cloak well, as Dumbledore instructed. They prepare for his final uses of it. He pulls it over himself on his way to the Great Hall,[141] as he prepares to confront Voldemort in the forest, echoing his first use of it. Then, putting on "his father's Cloak," he wanted to be alone.[142]

This time too he is alone, alone with his destiny. He reveals himself only to Neville, to make sure the last Horcrux is dealt with,[143] remaining hidden even from his love, Ginny.[144] Alone, he faces Voldemort: it is "just the two of them."[145] His final use of the cloak is to conceal his life:[146] Voldemort thinks he has already killed him. Pulling it off for his final confrontation with Voldemort, he announces loudly that only he must face Voldemort.[147] The cloak has hidden him so that he can do it alone. It is the means of his courage and his acceptance of responsibility. It is also the symbol of the humility that ultimately defeats pride. What is hidden and humble overcomes what proclaims itself and tries to dominate.

HOUSE~ELVES AND HUMILITY

The victory of learning humility belongs not only to the hidden Harry. At the final confrontation with Voldemort, the house-elves of Hogwarts swarm into the Entrance Hall to fight, "screaming and waving carving knives and cleavers."[148] They are so hidden in their way of life that Hermione, in her fourth year at Hogwarts, has never seen one, it being the mark of good house-elf that you don't know it is there.[149] It is a victory not just for humble wizards and house-elves, but also for the truth.

Humility is fundamentally truthfulness. The outward life of Voldemort is characterized by lies: the hidden life is characterized by the truth that is identified with the unseen God. The next chapter briefly considers this latter value.

Notes

1. *The Goblet of Fire*, 158.
2. *The Goblet of Fire*, 156.
3. *The Chamber of Secrets*, 232.
4. *The Chamber of Secrets*, 233.
5. *The Chamber of Secrets*, 235–36.
6. *The Chamber of Secrets*, 232.
7. *The Philosopher's Stone*, 88.
8. *The Order of the Phoenix*, 186–87.
9. *The Chamber of Secrets*, 235.
10. *The Deathly Hallows*, 586–87.
11. *The Chamber of Secrets*, 232.
12. *Merchant of Venice*, act 3, scene 2, line 131.

13. Isaiah 53:2–3.
14. *The Deathly Hallows*, 586.
15. *The Deathly Hallows*, 586.
16. *The Deathly Hallows*, 587.
17. *The Deathly Hallows*, 586.
18. *The Philosopher's Stone*, 71.
19. *The Philosopher's Stone*, 108.
20. *The Half-Blood Prince*, 165–66.
21. *The Half-Blood Prince*, 133.
22. *The Philosopher's Stone*, 198.
23. *The Deathly Hallows*, 587.
24. *The Deathly Hallows*, 606.
25. *The Imitation of Christ*, Book 1, chapter 2.
26. *The Philosopher's Stone*, 15–16.
27. *The Philosopher's Stone*, 15.
28. *The Philosopher's Stone*, 16.
29. *The Half-Blood Prince*, 57.
30. *The Order of the Phoenix*, 737.
31. *The Half-Blood Prince*, 259.
32. *The Philosopher's Stone*, 11.
33. *The Chamber of Secrets*, 91.
34. *The Deathly Hallows*, 387.
35. *The Goblet of Fire*, 73.
36. *The Chamber of Secrets*, 7–8.
37. *The Philosopher's Stone*, 223.
38. *The Philosopher's Stone*, 17–18.
39. *The Philosopher's Stone*, 101.
40. *The Chamber of Secrets*, 49.
41. *The Chamber of Secrets*, 50.
42. *The Chamber of Secrets*, 145–47.
43. *The Chamber of Secrets*, 151–52.
44. *The Deathly Hallows*, 572.
45. *The Philosopher's Stone*, 20.
46. *The Deathly Hallows*, 563.

47. *The Deathly Hallows*, 590.
48. *The Goblet of Fire*, 238.
49. *The Goblet of Fire*, 252.
50. *The Goblet of Fire*, 313.
51. *The Order of the Phoenix*, 269.
52. *The Order of the Phoenix*, 71.
53. *The Deathly Hallows*, 207–8.
54. *The Deathly Hallows*, 556.
55. *The Deathly Hallows*, 558–59.
56. *The Philosopher's Stone*, 212–13.
57. *The Goblet of Fire*, 15.
58. *The Goblet of Fire*, 555.
59. *The Deathly Hallows*, 562–63.
60. *The Deathly Hallows*, 596.
61. *The Chamber of Secrets*, 77.
62. *The Chamber of Secrets*, 220.
63. *The Chamber of Secrets*, 224.
64. *The Chamber of Secrets*, 78.
65. *The Chamber of Secrets*, 77.
66. *The Chamber of Secrets*, 218.
67. *The Goblet of Fire*, 310.
68. *The Goblet of Fire*, 254.
69. *The Goblet of Fire*, 313.
70. Luke 4:5–13.
71. Luke 4:9–12.
72. *The Deathly Hallows*, 306.
73. *The Deathly Hallows*, 307.
74. *The Deathly Hallows*, 607.
75. *The Order of the Phoenix*, 269.
76. Matthew 6:3.
77. *The Prisoner of Azkaban*, 165–66.
78. *The Prisoner of Azkaban*, 315.
79. *The Goblet of Fire*, 635.
80. Matthew 6:4.

81. *The Deathly Hallows*, 544.
82. *The Deathly Hallows*, 545.
83. *The Order of the Phoenix*, 569–71.
84. *The Deathly Hallows*, 17–18.
85. *The Half-Blood Prince*, 556.
86. *The Order of the Phoenix*, 469, and *The Deathly Hallows*, 574.
87. *The Chamber of Secrets*, 220.
88. *The Order of the Phoenix*, 323.
89. *The Order of the Phoenix*, chapter 28.
90. *The Order of the Phoenix*, 569.
91. *The Order of the Phoenix*, 571.
92. *The Deathly Hallows*, 542.
93. Psalm 51:3.
94. Matthew 5:3.
95. *The Deathly Hallows*, 544.
96. *The Deathly Hallows*, 545.
97. *The Deathly Hallows*, 308.
98. Psalm 51:3.
99. *The Deathly Hallows*, 308.
100. *The Order of the Phoenix*, 293.
101. *The Deathly Hallows*, 308.
102. *The Order of the Phoenix*, 306.
103. *The Goblet of Fire*, 169–70.
104. *The Goblet of Fire*, 582.
105. Colossians 3:3.
106. *The Goblet of Fire*, 570.
107. *The Deathly Hallows*, 331–32.
108. *The Deathly Hallows*, 337.
109. *The Deathly Hallows*, 332.
110. 1 John 4:8.
111. Revelation 20:14.
112. *The Deathly Hallows*, 333.
113. Luke 14:11.

114. *The Deathly Hallows*, 261.
115. *The Deathly Hallows*, 159.
116. 1 Corinthians 13:4–5.
117. *The Goblet of Fire*, 148.
118. *The Philosopher's Stone*, 148.
119. *The Philosopher's Stone*, 148.
120. *The Deathly Hallows*, 572.
121. *The Half-Blood Prince*, 606.
122. *The Deathly Hallows*, 572.
123. *The Deathly Hallows*, 332.
124. *The Deathly Hallows*, 556.
125. *The Deathly Hallows*, 574.
126. *The Deathly Hallows*, 599.
127. *The Deathly Hallows*, 600.
128. *The Philosopher's Stone*, 65.
129. *The Deathly Hallows*, 599.
130. Deuteronomy 30:15 (Revised Standard Version).
131. *The Deathly Hallows*, 599.
132. *The Philosopher's Stone*, 151–53.
133. *The Philosopher's Stone*, 197.
134. *The Philosopher's Stone*, chapter 17.
135. *The Prisoner of Azkaban*, 206.
136. *The Prisoner of Azkaban*, 240–42.
137. *The Order of the Phoenix*, 650–52.
138. *The Deathly Hallows*, 136–38.
139. *The Deathly Hallows*, 263–64.
140. *The Deathly Hallows*, chapter 17.
141. *The Deathly Hallows*, 556.
142. *The Philosopher's Stone*, 151.
143. *The Deathly Hallows*, 557–58.
144. *The Deathly Hallows*, 558–59.

145. *The Deathly Hallows*, 563.
146. *The Deathly Hallows*, 587.
147. *The Deathly Hallows*, 590.
148. *The Deathly Hallows*, 588.
149. *The Goblet of Fire*, 161.

9

Telling It Like It Is

THE STRUGGLE FOR TRUTH

Truth needs to be struggled for. Lee Jordan is an apt poster boy for this. His aptitude is hinted at early on, in a Quidditch match. Gryffindor is playing Slytherin in the final, and Jordan does not conceal his view of the Slytherins' behavior. When Professor McGonagall accuses him of being biased, he says, "I'm telling it like it is, Professor!"[1] He finds his mature role as anchorman of the radio program *Potterwatch*, where he fearlessly speaks out, not against the tricks of the Slytherins, but against the lies of Voldemort and his Death Eaters.[2] Nearly all the other programs follow Voldemort's line.[3] Lee Jordan reports the grim truth of wizard, goblin, and Muggle deaths.[4] Between the schoolchild rivalries of the Quidditch match that Lee commentates on and the deathly struggle with the lies and murder perpetrated by Voldemort, there is an intermediate phase in the Harry Potter story where allegiance to the truth is in question.

FUDGING THE TRUTH

Significantly, this intermediate phase begins at the end of the fourth book, which is where the story begins to be an adult one. It is as though JK is saying that part of adulthood is facing the truth and deciding which side one is on. The Minister of Magic, Cornelius Fudge, fails in this, as his name would lead us to expect. He fudges the issues. His earlier appearances in the series do not lead to an expectation of clarity of discernment. He has Hagrid taken off to prison, although he is innocent, simply because he feels he has "got to be seen doing something."[5] He fails to understand that Sirius Black is innocent.[6] He allows, apparently from cowardice, a Dementor to suck out Barty Crouch's soul, preventing him from telling the truth about Voldemort.[7] Following this, there is an angry discussion in which Fudge refuses "to believe that Voldemort could have risen."[8] Fudge is concerned that he would lose office if he follows Dumbledore's advice and removes the Dementors from Azkaban, and that his career would be ended if he followed Dumbledore's suggestion of sending envoys to the giants. Dumbledore tells him that he is blinded by love of the office that he holds.[9]

Accepting the truth depends on a certain disinterestedness, and Fudge does not have this. Attachment to his own political power prevents him from facing reality. He and Dumbledore come to "a parting of the ways." For them to walk the same way, Fudge would need to be working against Voldemort.[10] To do that, he has to accept that Voldemort is back. Locked in his own comfort zone, Fudge thinks that Voldemort "just can't be." Even the sight of the Dark Mark on Snape's arm is not enough to persuade him.[11] Dumbledore is very clear where he himself stands. "Cedric

Diggory was murdered by Lord Voldemort," he tells his school. He distances himself from the Ministry of Magic, which does not want this said. Realizing that parents of some of his pupils will be horrified by his announcement, he explains, "It is my belief that truth is generally preferable to lies."[12] In saying this, he is affirming a Christian value, based on the Decalogue.[13] He is also being courageous. He is distinguished from Fudge by not being ruled by fear.

WITNESSING TO THE TRUTH

The question that divides Fudge and Dumbledore—whether Voldemort has risen—remains central for the whole of the fifth book. This chronicles a sort of phony war with Voldemort before hostilities are openly engaged; the real struggle at this point is between those who believe that he has risen and those who do not. The Ministry of Magic, under the leadership of Fudge, belongs to the latter camp. Professor Umbridge is his agent at Hogwarts.[14] In her Defense against the Dark Arts class, she sidelines the whole issue of fighting against evil by making it a matter of theory.[15] Harry's reaction to her attempt to suppress the fact that Voldemort has returned shows him to be a brave warrior for truth. Umbridge asserts that it is a lie that Voldemort is back. Harry responds simply, "It is NOT a lie!" pointing out that he saw him and fought him. He is given a detention for this, and then multiplies it by standing up and saying that Voldemort killed Cedric Diggory.[16] His standing up for the truth when it is a life and death matter shows him to be a true pupil of Dumbledore, making his Headmaster's values his own.

Harry's heroism in facing Umbridge extends even to the shedding of his blood. His punishment in her detentions is to write repeatedly *I must not tell lies* with a magical quill that cuts the words into the back of his hand, drawing blood.[17] He is a martyr—the word means "witness"—to the truth.

PROFIT AND THE PRESS

Rita Skeeter's Quick Quotes Quill is, in its way, as punishing to the truth as the quill Dolores Umbridge uses for detentions.[18] The *Daily Prophet* serves not truth, but, as its name suggests, profit. As Rita Skeeter says, "The *Prophet* exists to sell itself."[19] In the process, people are hurt. The report about Harry's life gives him "a sick, burning feeling of shame in his stomach."[20] A report about Hagrid drives *him* into hiding.[21] A report about Hermione in *Witch Weekly* leads to her receiving hate mail, including undiluted Bubotuber pus and a cold look from Mrs. Weasley.[22] However, it is the report that describes Harry as "disturbed and dangerous"[23] that causes the greatest trouble in the struggle to convince the magical community of the truth of Voldemort's return. Although Hermione bottles up Rita's malice,[24] the *Daily Prophet*, under Fudge's influence, uses the report to turn Harry "into someone nobody will believe."[25] Rita Skeeter, however, is eventually pressed into service to tell the magical public the truth about Voldemort's return in the pages of the *Quibbler*.[26] This does a lot to convince people that Harry is telling the truth about Voldemort. Harry gets letters telling him so.[27]

Fellow pupils are convinced,[28] and Seamus, whose mother has been influenced by the *Daily Prophet*,[29] tells Harry, "I believe you. And I've sent a copy of that magazine to me mam."[30] The argument between Dumbledore and Fudge about whether Voldemort has returned is won definitively by Dumbledore after Voldemort appears in the

Ministry of Magic.[31] Following this, Dumbledore surveys Fudge magisterially and gives him instructions.[32] The press's campaign to suppress the truth of Voldemort's return ends once and for all when the *Sunday Prophet* announces his return on its front page.[33]

COURAGE AND TRUTH

Fudge's efforts to present Harry negatively are, however, mild compared to what happens when Voldemort has taken over the Ministry of Magic. Journalistic hints are replaced by posters announcing Harry's outcast status.[34] The editor of the *Quibbler*, who helped Harry oppose Fudge, finds himself unable to oppose Voldemort when his daughter, Luna, is kidnapped by the Death Eaters. The *Quibbler* carries Harry's picture, "emblazoned with the words *Undesirable Number One*, and captioned with the reward money." The editor betrays Harry to the Death Eaters in the hope of getting his daughter back.[35] The price of truth and loyalty has become too high. It takes great courage to be faithful to the truth. It is therefore appropriate to give the last word on this subject to the head of Gryffindor house ("where dwell the brave of heart")[36]—Professor McGonagall. Although she counseled Harry to be careful when dealing with Umbridge,[37] when she is confronted with the lies of Voldemort's Death Eaters, she is completely forthright. Faced with Alecto and Amycus Carrow—who make Umbridge look tame[38]—she identifies the link between lies, cowardice, and violence.

Alecto has pressed her Dark Mark to summon Lord Voldemort because she has seen Harry.[39] However, after she has been Stunned by Luna, and Harry has hidden under his cloak,[40] Amycus finds himself in the position of expecting

Voldemort imminently without being able to justify summoning him. Harry apparently is no longer there. Amycus says, "We can push it off on the kids....We'll say they forced her to press her Mark, and that's why he got a false alarm....He can punish them. Couple of kids more or less, what's the difference?" Professor McGonagall's reply is magisterial: "Only the difference between truth and lies, courage and cowardice," she says, "a difference, in short, which you and your sister seem unable to appreciate," and she forbids Amycus to blame the students of Hogwarts.[41] In saying this, Professor McGonagall is articulating a key value that Harry has been learning while in her house at Hogwarts: the courageous acceptance of the truth. This is a fundamental Christian value, since truth is God's will as expressed to us in what actually happens. The devil, who opposes God's will, is "the father of lies."[42] Harry's story shows that living by truth is costly. He learns it not as something merely academic—it is significant that Umbridge's "theory-centered" lessons are of this nature[43]—but as something the acquisition of which demands a real exposure to adversity and opposition.

Harry's whole story documents the cost of the struggle for truth. He suffers because he is a wizard, and the Dursleys do not want to acknowledge this aspect of reality.[44] He suffers because he is untruthfully taken to be the heir of Slytherin.[45] He suffers because Pettigrew conceals who he really is and Black has to conceal who he is because of Pettigrew's lies.[46] He suffers because it is wrongly supposed that he put his name in the Goblet of Fire.[47] He suffers because Voldemort deceives him into thinking that Sirius is at the Ministry,[48] and as a result of his going there on this assumption, Sirius is drawn there and is killed.[49] He suffers because he is wrongly identified as a public enemy.[50] He suffers because Voldemort lies that he permits his friends to die rather than to face Voldemort himself.[51] His suffering, bravely borne, leads to the triumph of the truth.

UNFOLDING THE TRUTH

The Harry Potter story is the unfolding of the truth. A lot of its narrative power comes from the surprise with which each new revelation is greeted. Its revelations are in a sense an anticipation of the last judgment, when, as Jesus warns his disciples, "Whatever you have said in the dark will be heard in the light, and what you have whispered behind closed doors will be proclaimed from the house-tops."[52] It shows people courageously taking the side of truth, as Harry and his friends do, or taking the side of lies, as Lockhart with his pathetic fantasies and the Carrows with their repulsive ignorance do. It shows—through the *Daily Prophet*—that it is not enough just to want to serve the market to be on the side of truth, and—through the *Quibbler*—that even a stand in favor of the truth is not invulnerable to pressure.

However, although in the clarity of the final judgment of the complete series it is clear who is on which side, within the narrative it remains unclear. Reputation is no guide, as the reader is continually reminded in an astonishing series of reversals where the colors of good and evil are run down and the opposite run up as battle is engaged and the wisdom of the gospel injunction not to judge is once more shown.[53] Sirius is painted very black, so that his gift of a Firebolt is suspected of malevolence.[54] The suspicion of the identity of the giver is correct,[55] but the intentions of the giver are completely misjudged. An opposite misjudgment is made about Crouch junior pretending to be Moody. His apparently benevolent help is shown to be malevolent.[56]

And Snape is so little understood that by the end of Harry's sixth year none of the other characters still alive believe that he is against Voldemort. The story makes clear that truth in this world is not clearly labeled, simply awaiting allegiance.

Life is lived amidst a tangle of truth and lies, without any guarantee that it will be clear which is which before this life is ended. Yet truth is to be sought. Whatever happens in the world, it is not a doomed quest, because truth can be found in the heart. The truth of God can be found in the heart. The Sermon on the Mount teaches that to be pure in heart is to see God.[57] This ultimate Christian goal is put before the reader of the Harry Potter stories, and its consideration in the next chapter completes our look at the spiritual values in them.

Notes

1. *The Prisoner of Azkaban*, 226–27.
2. *The Deathly Hallows*, 355–60.
3. *The Deathly Hallows*, 355.
4. *The Deathly Hallows*, 356.
5. *The Chamber of Secrets*, 193.
6. *The Prisoner of Azkaban*, 285.
7. *The Goblet of Fire*, 610.
8. *The Goblet of Fire*, 613.
9. *The Goblet of Fire*, 614.
10. *The Goblet of Fire*, 615.
11. *The Goblet of Fire*, 616.
12. *The Goblet of Fire*, 626.
13. Deuteronomy 5:20.
14. *The Order of the Phoenix*, 193.
15. *The Order of the Phoenix*, 220.
16. *The Order of the Phoenix*, 221.
17. *The Order of the Phoenix*, 241.

18. *The Goblet of Fire*, 266.
19. *The Order of the Phoenix*, 501.
20. *The Goblet of Fire*, 276.
21. *The Goblet of Fire*, 380–82; 384–85; 392–95.
22. *The Goblet of Fire*, 444–45; 470; 537.
23. *The Goblet of Fire*, 531.
24. *The Goblet of Fire*, 630–32.
25. *The Order of the Phoenix*, 71.
26. *The Order of the Phoenix*, 502.
27. *The Order of the Phoenix*, 511.
28. *The Order of the Phoenix*, 514.
29. *The Order of the Phoenix*, 196–97.
30. *The Order of the Phoenix*, 514.
31. *The Order of the Phoenix*, 716.
32. *The Order of the Phoenix*, 722.
33. *The Order of the Phoenix*, 745–46.
34. *The Deathly Hallows*, 208.
35. *The Order of the Phoenix*, 340.
36. *The Philosopher's Stone*, 88.
37. *The Order of the Phoenix*, 223.
38. *The Deathly Hallows*, 461.
39. *The Deathly Hallows*, 473.
40. *The Deathly Hallows*, 474.
41. *The Deathly Hallows*, 477.
42. John 8:44.
43. *The Order of the Phoenix*, 216.
44. *The Chamber of Secrets*, 7–8.
45. *The Chamber of Secrets*, 148–52.
46. *The Prisoner of Azkaban*, chapters 17 and 18.
47. *The Goblet of Fire*, 252.
48. *The Order of the Phoenix*, 641.
49. *The Order of the Phoenix*, 711.
50. *The Deathly Hallows*, 340.
51. *The Deathly Hallows*, 529.

52. Luke 12:3.
53. Matthew 7:1.
54. *The Prisoner of Azkaban*, 172.
55. *The Prisoner of Azkaban*, 315.
56. *The Goblet of Fire*, 587–89.
57. Matthew 5:8.

10

They Will See God

PURITY OF HEART AND
PURITY OF BLOOD

John Cassian is a highly influential figure in the history of monastic life. In its early years, he sat at the feet of wise old men in the Egyptian desert and listened. He brought their wisdom back to Europe and published it in a series of "conferences." The first of these spiritual talks explains the objective of every monk. It is purity of heart. "Everything we do…," it explains, "must be undertaken for the sake of this purity of heart."[1] Only in this way will the monk realize the promise of the gospel, "Blessed are the pure in heart, for they will see God."[2] By sincerely wanting what is true and good in the depth of his heart, the monk reaches the king-dom of God[3] —simply to want God sincerely is to find him, since he cannot be outdone in love.

TRUE DESIRE

JK presents this ancient teaching afresh for new generations through Harry's story. In his sixth year at Hogwarts, Dumbledore says to him:

> "In spite of all the temptation you have endured, all the suffering, you remain pure of heart, just as pure as you were at the age of eleven, when you stared into a mirror that reflected your heart's desire, and it showed you only the way to thwart Voldemort, and not immortality or riches."[4]

Harry's Headmaster is referring to the Mirror of Erised, which reflects desire—its name is the letters of the word *desire* reversed, as they would be reflected in a mirror. He explains to Harry in his first year at Hogwarts that "it shows us nothing more or less than the deepest, most desperate desire of our hearts."[5] Harry remembers this when he finds himself confronting Quirrell, who has been possessed by Voldemort. He hears Quirrell murmuring that the "Mirror is the key to finding the Stone." He thinks, "What I want more than anything else in the world at the moment…is to find the Stone before Quirrell does. So if I look in the Mirror, I should see myself finding it—which means I'll see where it's hidden!" This is what happens—the Mirror shows him taking the stone out of his pocket and putting it back there, at which moment it really does drop into his pocket.[6]

The Mirror reflects Harry's true desire, and because he truly wants to thwart Voldemort, he is able to see how he can do so. Any wizard whose true desire was for immortality or riches would not have seen the stone. Afterward, Dumbledore explains the protective magic of the Mirror to Harry: "Only one who wanted to *find* the Stone—find it, but not use it—would be able to get it, otherwise they'd just see themselves making gold or drinking Elixir of Life."[7] Harry is pure of heart because he is not diverted from his goal of fighting evil by advantage for himself. Through this purity of heart he can confront evil and not be overcome by it. The heart is the battleground. Harry's best weapon against Voldemort is "the incomparable power of a soul that is untarnished and whole."[8] The true struggle is interior.

PURE-BLOODEDNESS AND PREJUDICE

Neither Voldemort nor the tradition he comes from, nor Fudge, nor Umbridge, see it this way. Their view of what matters is more exterior. For purity of heart, they substitute purity of blood. This has echoes of the Nazi regime's concern for Aryan blood and the concomitant murderous discrimination, but the more fundamental point that JK seems to be making is that concern about one's outward circumstances can never replace the inward spiritual journey. This is apparent in what Dumbledore says to Fudge just after Crouch junior has had his soul sucked out:

> "You place too much importance, and you always have done, on the so-called purity of blood! You fail to recognize that it matters not what someone is born, but what they grow to be! Your Dementor has just destroyed the last remaining member of a pure-blood family as old as any—and see what that man chose to make of his life!"[9]

Harry first hears the bad word that expresses this attitude in his second Hogwarts year, when Malfoy calls Hermione a "filthy little Mudblood."[10] In doing this, Malfoy is reflecting the attitude of Malfoy senior, whom Harry overhears telling Draco that he should be ashamed that "a girl of no wizard family" beats him in every exam. For Lucius Malfoy, as is clear from the conversation with Mr. Borgin that follows this, wizard blood matters.[11]

Hagrid explains both the insult and the attitude:

> "Mudblood's a really foul name for some who was Muggle-born—you know, non-magic parents. There are some wizards—like Malfoy's family— who think they're better than everyone else because they're what people call pure-blood."[12]

As Ron points out, the idea of blood being dirty doesn't make sense because, "Most wizards these days are half-blood anyway. If we hadn't married Muggles we'd have died out."[13] Inbreeding is not healthy. Voldemort comes from "a very ancient wizarding family noted for a vein of instability and violence that flourished through the generations through their habit of marrying their own cousins."[14] The excessive emphasis on wizard blood of the Malfoys and their ilk mirrors the Dursleys' excessive emphasis on being "perfectly normal, thank you very much."[15] This attitude, announced in the first sentence of the series, is really the same as that of the wizards obsessed with being pure-blood: it is a prejudice against people who are different. The spiritually healthy attitude is one that accepts others. This attitude characterizes both Hermione's parents, who go into Gringotts to change their Muggle money, and Mr. Weasley who greets them there delightedly, saying, "But you're *Muggles!*...We must have a drink!"[16]

THE BATTLE BETWEEN ACCEPTANCE AND DISCRIMINATION

In one sense, the Harry Potter story is a story of the struggle between two attitudes: that which accepts others in their differences, and that which does not. The Dursleys, Fudge, Umbridge, and Voldemort are all defeated by the more generous, loving attitude that wants to welcome others. This is symbolized by the arrangement in the final gathering in the Great Hall:

> Nobody was sitting according to house any more: all were jumbled together, teachers and pupils, ghosts and parents, centaurs and house-elves, and Firenze lay recovering in a corner, and Grawp peered in through a smashed window, and people were throwing food into his laughing mouth.[17]

All manner of prejudice is overcome here. Fudge had said earlier of the giants, "People hate them."[18] Grawp's inclusion is a triumph of the spirit that welcomes otherness. Umbridge had called centaurs "filthy half-breeds."[19] Their presence shows that her view does not prevail. Muggle-born Hermione, on the other hand, is vindicated by the acceptance of house-elves into the gathering.

Prejudice is the projection of the impure heart. The darkness within is fastened on others. The sense of the need for purity is refocused from the purity of one's own heart, where it properly belongs, onto the purity of others. This is the drift of the Black family motto *Toujours Pur* (meaning, in French, "always pure").[20] It is clearly not a pure heart that shrieks, "*Filth! Scum! By-products of dirt and vileness! Half-breeds, mutants, freaks!*"[21] The impurity of the heart is poured out on those designated to receive it. The issue of whether to project the inner darkness like this, or (the implicit alternative) to struggle for purity of heart as Cassian teaches, is foundational to the history of Hogwarts' troubles. It begins with Slytherin, which "took only pure-blood wizards"[22] and which thought "magical learning should be kept within all-magic families."[23]

Gryffindor disagrees. There is dueling and fighting that only ends with the departure of Slytherin, breaking the harmony that initially existed among the school's founders.[24] There is a legend that Slytherin's heir "would be able to unseal the Chamber of Secrets, unleash the horror within, and use it to purge the school of all who were unworthy to study magic."[25] Tom Riddle, whose grandfather proudly announces that the family is Salazar Slytherin's last living descendants,[26] takes on the role through his diary Horcrux.[27] Harry (whose grandfather was in Gryffindor)[28] is given the sword of Godric Gryffindor through the Sorting Hat, and with it he kills the Basilisk that comes out of the mouth of the stone statue of Slytherin.[29] In being given and wielding the sword that has the name of the founder of his house engraved on it,[30] Harry shows himself to be as much an heir of Gryffindor as Riddle (calling himself Voldemort)[31] is of Slytherin. His status as Gryffindor's heir is confirmed when Scrimgeour announces that Dumbledore's will bequeaths him "the sword of Godric Gryffindor."[32] His fight with Voldemort is a continuation of Gryffindor's fight with Slytherin.

We are, in effect, being shown a battle that has been going on for over a thousand years—the professor of the History of Magic dates the founding wizards and witches of Hogwarts that far back.[33] The implication is that the struggle between the two attitudes of discrimination (Slytherin) and acceptance (Gryffindor) is an almost primordial one. It is a struggle between a refusal to love and a willingness to love. More deeply, it is a struggle between the esteeming of outward purity and the esteeming of inward purity—purity of heart. Placing the burden of purity outside of oneself leads to murder, as is clear from Voldemort's career; placing the burden of purity inside oneself leads to the capacity to love, as is clear from Harry's "ability to love," which Dumbledore explicitly links to his remaining "pure of heart."[34] Purity of heart is needed to love—otherwise the heart's impurities are projected onto others. That is why purity of heart is the goal of the monk.

THE POWER OF A PURE HEART

Purity of heart is a matter of life and death. It is the way to liberation not just for wizardkind but for all magical creatures. So much is implied by the effect of its opponent, Voldemort. The house-elf Dobby worships Harry because it was through him (as a baby) that Voldemort fell. Dobby says to him:

> "Ah, if Harry Potter only knew!…If he knew what he means to us, to the lowly, the enslaved, us dregs of the magical world! Dobby remembers how it was when He Who Must Not Be Named was at the height of his powers, sir! We house-elfs were treated like vermin, sir!"[35]

When Voldemort rises again and takes over the Ministry, the persecution of Muggle-borns begins. They are accused of obtaining magical power "by theft or force."[36] They are excluded from Hogwarts.[37] They are rounded up and interviewed by the "Muggle-born Registration Commission."[38] The head of this sinister body is Dolores Umbridge.[39] It produces pamphlets entitled *Mudbloods and the Dangers They Pose to a Peaceful Pure-Blood Society*.[40] The one who is different is demonized rather than loved. A pure-blood society is a society that is not pure-hearted. Only the pure of heart can avoid being drawn into some kind of discrimination, whether through projection of the darkness within or in the hope of some partial advantage. It is therefore of the essence that Harry, whose mission is to defeat the pure-blood society in the person of Voldemort, should be pure of heart. Purity of heart confronts and overcomes the ethos of purity of blood. This is the drama of Hogwarts and the drama of Harry's story.

THE INNER BATTLE

However, Harry's story is not just an outward drama between opposing forces: it is also an inward drama. The theme of this conflict is replayed within the soul of a single individual: Severus Snape. As Harry discovers through accidentally sharing his worst memory, Snape has a very damaged heart.[41] Within it, the drama of the conflict between purity of heart and the ethos of purity of blood is played out. The struggle begins when Snape is just a boy. He is asked by Lily Evans, whose parents are Muggles, "Does it make a difference, being Muggle-born?" This is for Snape the mother of all questions. His whole life revolves around it. Within him is played out the conflict that takes place first between Slytherin and Gryffindor, and finally between Voldemort and Harry. Snape hesitates when asked the question. It seems his answer is swayed by love, for "his black eyes, eager in the greenish gloom," move "over the pale face, the dark red hair" of Lily, his love. The loving answer comes: "No....It doesn't make any difference." He reassures her, "You've got loads of magic."[42] He almost forgets this, however, on their first Hogwarts Express journey, when he says of Petunia, "She's only a—" before catching himself quickly.[43]

Lily asks him to come with her to another compartment away from James Potter and Sirius Black, but the ancient quarrel between Slytherin and Gryffindor is fated to divide them: she joins James and Sirius in Gryffindor's house, while the Sorting Hat puts Severus into Slytherin's. Lily does not like the Dark Magic of Severus's new companions.[44] The turning point in their relationship, however, comes when Severus has been humiliated by James and Sirius, and Lily comes to his defense. James taunts him with the fact that he was rescued by her, and Snape retorts, "I don't need help from filthy little Mudbloods like her!"[45] This dooms Severus to rejection by Lily. It is no good apologizing to her, saying, "I never meant to call you Mudblood!" She knows he associates with Death Eaters and calls everyone of her birth Mudblood: it is the parting of their ways.[46]

The break between Severus and Lily mirrors the break between Slytherin and Gryffindor, whose friendship, like theirs, was once "firm and true."[47] Unlike Slytherin, though, Snape does not simply abandon his friend. He wants to defend her from Voldemort and offers Dumbledore anything in return for help with this. When Voldemort kills her anyway, he promises Dumbledore that he will help look after Harry.[48] In doing this, Severus shows that purity of heart is possible even for one who has been deeply involved in the purity of blood ethos. In fact, it could be argued that he is not only the bravest of men, as Harry tells his son named for him,[49] but also the purest-hearted of men. This is so because the love that motivates him is so hidden. There is nothing in what he receives from other people—except Dumbledore, and this is lost when he kills him[50]—that gives him any affirmation or return for what he chooses to do, certainly not a happy relationship with Lily's son. Lily is dead; there is only love left, and that is, always, hidden in Severus's heart.[51]

HOPE FOR THE HUMAN HEART

In telling us Severus's story, JK is telling a story of Christian hope. Even one who grew up so conspicuously lacking "that indefinable air of having been well cared for,"[52] even one who has allowed Voldemort to burn the Dark Mark into his arm to distinguish him as a Death Eater,[53] even one who has lost all earthly hope of his love being reciprocated—even such a one as this can be true to love to the very end, risking and ultimately sacrificing all for the overthrow of its enemy.[54] Of all the plot reversals in the Harry Potter books—and, of course, there are many—perhaps none is as surprising as the discovery that Severus Snape can be described by these words of the Sermon on the Mount: "Blessed are the pure in heart, for they will see God."[55] Severus's story says that the human heart can change. In the last year of his life, the former housemaster of Slytherin forbids his fellow Slytherin Phineas Nigellus[56] to use the word *Mudblood*.[57] It is the triumph of purity of heart over the ethos of purity of blood.

Severus Snape and Harry Potter are twinned in their involvement in this triumph. Severus fights it without being seen by others; Harry, ultimately, fights it in the gaze of a "watching crowd."[58] The triumph of purity of heart frames the entire series. In Severus's case it begins with his muttering a countercurse to save Harry from plunging off his broom during a Quidditch match,[59] and it ends with his giving Harry his memories,[60] so that Harry knows what he has to do to defeat the one whose murderous intent is the imposition of purity of blood.[61] For one second Snape looks into Harry's eyes, seeing in them the living continuation of his beloved; this second—his last in this world—marks the triumph of his love for Harry's mother over his hatred for his father, the triumph of purity of heart.[62] In Harry's case, this begins when he can see the Philosopher's Stone in the Mirror of Erised because he wants to find it to defeat Voldemort more than he wants gold or long life,[63] and it ends when, happy to have defeated Voldemort, he puts the Elder Wand back where it came from, his heart free from the trouble of power.[64] He has reached the objective of the life of every monk. This is the final triumph of purity of heart.

However, it is not the end of the story. JK reminds us in the epilogue that there is another generation. They too will have to learn purity of heart if they are to see God. It is a reminder that spiritual values have always to be learned anew, struggled for anew. James, Albus, Lily, Hugo, and Rose have a lot to learn, but they have Harry's story to help them. So do we. And so do our children.

Notes

1. John Cassian, *John Cassian: Conferences*, translated by Colm Luibheid (New York / Mahwah, NJ: Paulist Press, 1985), 41.

2. Matthew 5:8.

3. *John Cassian: Conferences*, 39.

4. *The Half-Blood Prince*, 477–78.

5. *The Philosopher's Stone*, 157.

6. *The Philosopher's Stone*, 210–12.

7. *The Philosopher's Stone*, 217.

8. *The Half-Blood Prince*, 478.

9. *The Goblet of Fire*, 614–15.

10. *The Chamber of Secrets*, 86.

11. *The Chamber of Secrets*, 44.

12. *The Chamber of Secrets*, 89.

13. *The Chamber of Secrets*, 89.

14. *The Half-Blood Prince*, 200–201.

15. *The Philosopher's Stone*, 8.

16. *The Chamber of Secrets*, 47.

17. *The Deathly Hallows*, 597.

18. *The Goblet of Fire*, 614.

19. *The Order of the Phoenix*, 665.

20. *The Deathly Hallows*, 155.

21. *The Order of the Phoenix*, 74.

22. *The Order of the Phoenix*, 185.

23. *The Chamber of Secrets*, 114.

24. *The Order of the Phoenix*, 186.

25. *The Chamber of Secrets*, 114.

26. *The Half-Blood Prince*, 196.

27. *The Chamber of Secrets*, chapter 17.

28. *The Deathly Hallows*, 539.

29. *The Chamber of Secrets*, 235–36.

30. *The Chamber of Secrets*, 245.

31. *The Chamber of Secrets*, 231.

32. *The Deathly Hallows*, 109.

33. *The Chamber of Secrets*, 114.

34. *The Half-Blood Prince*, 477–78.

35. *The Chamber of Secrets*, 133.

36. *The Deathly Hallows*, 172.

37. *The Deathly Hallows*, 173.

38. *The Deathly Hallows*, 172.

39. *The Deathly Hallows*, 206.

40. *The Deathly Hallows*, 205.

41. *The Order of the Phoenix*, 563–72.

42. *The Deathly Hallows*, 535.

43. *The Deathly Hallows*, 538.

44. *The Deathly Hallows*, 539–40.

45. *The Order of the Phoenix*, 569–71.

46. *The Deathly Hallows*, 542.
47. *The Order of the Phoenix*, 186.
48. *The Deathly Hallows*, 543–45.
49. *The Deathly Hallows*, 607.
50. *The Half-Blood Prince*, 556.
51. *The Deathly Hallows*, 552.
52. *The Deathly Hallows*, 538.
53. *The Goblet of Fire*, 616.
54. *The Deathly Hallows*, 528.
55. Matthew 5:8.
56. *The Deathly Hallows*, 598.
57. *The Deathly Hallows*, 553.
58. *The Deathly Hallows*, 591.
59. *The Philosopher's Stone*, 209.
60. *The Deathly Hallows*, 528.
61. *The Deathly Hallows*, chapter 33.
62. *The Deathly Hallows*, 528.
63. *The Philosopher's Stone*, 212.
64. *The Deathly Hallows*, 600.